GREE
GHOSTS, GHOULS & UNSOLVED MYSTERIES

GREEN MOUNTAIN GHOSTS, GHOULS & UNSOLVED MYSTERIES

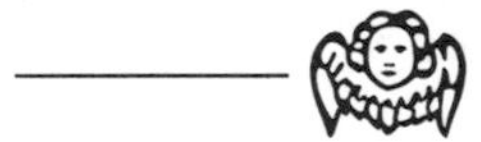

Joseph A. Citro

Illustrations by Bonnie Christensen

Foreword by Howard Frank Mosher

Houghton Mifflin Company
Boston New York

For information about permission to reproduce selections from this book, write to
Permissions, Houghton Mifflin Company,
215 Park Avenue South,
New York, New York 10003.

Library of Congress Cataloging-in-Publication Data

Citro, Joseph A.
Green mountain ghosts, ghouls & unsolved mysteries / Joseph A. Citro;
illustrations by Bonnie Christensen; foreword by Howard Frank Mosher.
p. cm.
ISBN 1-881527-51-4 — ISBN 1-881527-50-6
1. Folklore—Vermont. 2. Folklore—Vermont—Green Mountains.
I. Title. II. Title: Green mountain ghosts, ghouls, and unsolved mysteries.
GR110.V4C57 1994 94-25962
398'.09743—dc20

Printed and bound in Canada by
Best Book Manufacturers, Inc.

Designed by Eugenie Seidenberg Delaney

10 9 8 7 6

This book is for
Rod, Holly, Brian and Allison—
my family.

CONTENTS

Foreword

By Howard Frank Mosher

When I first settled in Vermont's Green Mountains thirty years ago, I knew immediately that I'd discovered a last New England frontier. Here were magnificent, unspoiled lakes and rivers, extensive forests still wild enough to become hopelessly lost in, some of the most independent-minded and self-sufficient people left on the face of the Earth, and—best of all, so far as I was concerned—hundreds of wonderful stories just waiting to be written. Every hill farmer and horse logger and old-time hunter and trapper seemed to have dozens of spellbinding tales to tell. As an apprentice storyteller myself, I felt as though I'd struck a bonanza.

Many of the stories I heard involved mysteries, and a good number of these mysteries touched on the supernatural. A week or so after I arrived in Vermont, my landlady mentioned to me that she'd just learned of the tragic death in a car accident of her first cousin. Quite matter-of-factly, she added, "I wasn't greatly surprised. Last night my closet door opened and shut itself three times. I knew right then that someone in the family was going to die."

I'll admit that I was skeptical. Yet how could I totally discount anything told to me by this intelligent, kind, tough-minded woman who, I would learn later, had saved her family farm during the Depression by working side by side with her husband in the barn and the fields for twelve and fourteen hours a day and then, under the cover of darkness, manufacturing moonshine whiskey to pay the mortgage?

Not long afterward, a boy from a neighboring farm took me trout fishing on a remote mountain brook. When we came to a deep pool at the bottom of a falls, he remarked that about a year ago, he'd waked up in the night to see, standing sopping wet in an unearthly light at the foot of his bed, a strange young boy. The following morning, when he told his mother about the visitation, she turned pale, then showed him an old photograph of the same boy—who, it turned out, was an uncle who had drowned years ago in the very pool we were fishing.

As time passed, I learned of stranger matters still: inexplicable disappearances in the big woods near the Canadian border, acts of violence and madness more bone-chilling than anything you'd read in the wildest supermarket tabloids, mysterious sightings in Vermont's skies and waters. By degrees, I became less skeptical about some of these tales. Just maybe, there were more things in the Green Mountains than had previously been dreamed of in my philosophy. At the very least, it would behoove me, as a budding writer, to keep an open mind about such matters.

Now, in *Green Mountain Ghosts, Ghouls & Unsolved Mysteries*, the acclaimed novelist Joseph A. Citro has chronicled scores of Vermont's unique tales of the occult and much, much more. Born and raised in the Green Mountains himself, Joe Citro has, by his own admission, "courted the bizarre, the grotesque and the mysterious for more than thirty years." The result is this splendid gallery of spine-tingling and original ghost stories, historical events as little-known as they are horrific, profiles of surpassingly outrageous Vermont characters, and numerous inexplicable happenings, from repeated sightings of a flying silo to the putative appearances, down through the centuries, of Lake Champlain's own resident sea serpent, "Champ." Little wonder that for many years, Vermont was a prime source of material for P.T. Barnum's sideshows and Robert Ripley's "Believe It or Not" column.

Here, in one vastly entertaining wonder book are tales not only of haunted houses, but haunted colleges, bodies of water and even a haunted covered bridge; prodigies such as Zera Colburn, the 6-year-old mathematical genius from Cabot, and the Eddy brothers, Vermont's own pioneering spiritualists, who routinely baffled the toughest investigative reporters of the day; the fanatical Millerites, who donned flowing white "ascension robes" and clambered up to the tops of hills all over New England in glorious expectation of the imminent end of the world; not to mention Vermont's own elite corps of professional grave robbers.

Most frightening of all are Mr. Citro's investigations into the realm of grim *human* events. It's all too easy to forget, in these days of miracle drugs, the terrible killer plague known as the White Death that claimed hundreds of Vermonters a year as recently as a century ago, and the resulting vampire scares in such bastions of Green Mountain respectability as Woodstock and Manchester. Then there's the almost unspeakably bizarre killing, unsolved to this day, of the hard-working Upper Connecticut Valley dairy farmer, and, in the mountains near Bennington, the vanishing into thin air of half a dozen persons from 1945 to 1950.

As those of us familiar with *The Unseen*, *Dark Twilight* and Joseph A. Citro's other popular suspense novels have long known, Mr. Citro is blessed with a wonderfully distinctive storytelling voice—lucid, speculative, gently iconoclastic—just the sort of reliable nonjudgmental voice you'd *want* to tell you a ghost story. Some of the more outlandish tales in the book he demystifies with the pungent wit for which Vermonters are justly fabled. For others, he suggests possible or partial explanations. Still others he simply reports as he heard them in the hundreds of interviews he conducted from the Canadian border to the Massachusetts' state line. Above all, the impression he leaves us with is that, yes, genuine mysteries still do lurk out there in those mountains, and many of them will never be fully explained.

When it comes to Vermont's tales of the occult, even the most skeptical of us can be given pause. One of my favorite chapters in this book recounts the tale of a grave in Middlebury containing a body laid to rest in. 1883—1883 *B.C.* that is! (No, it doesn't contain a Native American.)

Impossible? That's what I thought, at first. But I was wrong. The story of Vermont's 3,375-year-old corpse is almost certainly true, and it's perfectly well authenticated.

How can such a thing possibly be? Read on in *Green Mountain Ghosts, Ghouls & Unsolved Mysteries*. If you delight in "the bizarre, the grotesque and the mysterious," you're in for a rare treat.

Introduction

THE FOLLOWING ARE TALES OF VERMONTERS and—as artist and humorist Francis Colburn once said—the odd state that they're in. Vermont-born myself, I have courted the bizarre, the grotesque and the mysterious for more than thirty years. In the process, I have collected enough strange-but-true and strange-but-*maybe*-true stories to fill this book; the spillover could fill a second volume this size.

And still I suspect I've only scratched the surface of our Green Mountain mysteries.

This curio collecting is an odd hobby, I admit, and people have wondered why I do it.

Some have asked me why I write such—(here they pause, looking for a euphemism) . . . unusual novels?

And, they ask, whatever would possess me to offer such . . . unorthodox commentary on Vermont Public Radio?

Now, with the publication of this book, those same folks will probably wonder why I'd want to put together an outlandish collection of oddities such as this?

The answer is simple: because the history of Vermont is made up of terrific stories. And our folklore has outlasted any best seller you can name.

In my years at the keyboard, I've come to realize that most people don't see Vermont exactly the way I do. They don't see it as a scary place. For many, Vermont is a sort of Yankee Shangri-La, a romantic anachronism of color-changing hills, postcard-perfect villages and bright blue skies (pungent, no doubt, with the scent of maple syrup). It's simple and uncluttered, like the sunny seasonal covers of *Vermont Life* Magazine.

While romantics admire our white church steeples, I worry about what's lurking in their shadows. While idealists revere the purity of our crystal waters, I wonder what unknown creatures hide below the surface. While perspiring utopians tromp the trails of our forested state parks, I fret about the alien animals waiting just beyond the tree line.

Shadows. Shades. Things unseen. Wonders not yet defined or catalogued. It's the *other side* of Vermont—the darker side.

But light or dark, I'd never presume to say which perception is more accurate. My guess is they're symbiotic, that the clearest vision encompasses both. And if that is so, one might look around fearfully and conclude that what we call reality is a flimsy facade indeed.

The same you-can't-get-there-from-here Vermonter, a crusty old coot with his legendary reserve and abundant common sense, will be quick to tell you his well was the result of a dowser's handiwork. Then he'll puff thoughtfully on his corncob and recollect how there's something a mite peculiar about that abandoned house just down this side of Cy Sweeney's junkyard.

Why *do* I do it?

It's in my blood, I guess.

My grandfather came to Vermont to work on the railroad. I have distant memories of him, blurry with pipe smoke, relaxing in his armchair beside the kerosene heater. He was stereotypically down-to-earth. Never talked much, but when he spoke, he would sometimes recall deaths and suicides and the strange things he had seen at night when he walked the tracks with his lantern.

My father was a storyteller. When I was small he told me how, during a fierce electrical storm, a fiery globe of light had chased him through the house.

And how, as a boy, he had concealed himself in an orchard to watch a family of deer grow intoxicated by munching fallen apples.

And how he had seen an enigmatic wispy shape—a ghost, perhaps?—floating silently downhill, gliding just above the ground, and the trees had parted to let it pass . . .

All fantasy, right? Every word a fiction.

Later, I learned that ball lightning exists and can behave much as my father described. Maybe it really *did* chase him around the house.

And deer *do* become tipsy when they binge on fermenting apples.

But it's the last story that troubles me. Could it be true? Could something like that white soaring specter really exist?

Who can say?

And who can say where the following stories come from? Or why they stay around for so long.

Some are based on fact. Some *are* fact. And some, though they've passed the test of time, are total fabrication. I'll let the folklorists and historians do the sorting. All I know is that Vermonters—and would-be Vermonters—have always possessed an appetite for the bizarre. In that way, I suppose, Vermonters are just like everybody else.

In Plymouth, at Boy Scout Camp, we told stories of the purple hand. Clustered around the campfire, we all *knew* those discolored fingers were out there, just beyond the fading circle of firelight, impatiently clenching and unclenching. We knew sometime before morning one of us would feel that hand, cold and clammy as a trout, twitching inside his sleeping bag.

And later, in the utter darkness, whispering and waiting for sleep to come, we'd speculate that one of the gnarled and ancient trees nearby would pull itself from the ground and spider along on its roots in search of a midnight snack.

And long before that . . .

A circle of loggers camping in the Northeast Kingdom before it was the Northeast Kingdom. Another campfire, its dying light failing to keep the darkness at bay. Another cycle of stories. They talk about the men that have been lost to the river. They recall the storekeeper—funny acting fella—who snapped one night, axed his wife and kids. Then slept with them all together in the same bed.

What could possess a man to do such a thing?

Eyes on the dying flames, their discussion ends with the final, "Who can say . . . ?"

And the wind howls.

Or is it the wind?

Fictions. Stories. Myths. It all started long before that mysterious too-bright light in the sky turned out to be Venus.

And so what if that wispy specter among the trees is nothing but a wind-driven sheet escaping a neighbor's clothesline? What's to be afraid of? We knew it all the time.

But change can go the other way. Fact—every once in a while—can turn into fantasy. When I was in junior high school, it was a fact that no Indians had ever lived in Vermont. Today, archaeologists tell a different story: Native Americans have lived here for 10,000 years. The people Samuel de Champlain saw in 1609 were the *real* native Vermonters. Ethan Allen and his cronies were nothing but a bunch of land-grabbing flatlanders.

And speaking of Champlain, my schoolteachers told me he was the first European to set foot in Vermont. Most likely that too is apocryphal.

All the stories in this book are *real*. They may not all be *true*—or not exactly. For the most part you won't find them in television documentaries. They're not taught in our classrooms; they won't be filed and footnoted by our historians or indexed in our history texts.

They are full of frustrating phrases like: "It is said that . . ."; "I heard one time that . . ."; and, "A friend of my uncle's told me . . ."

But then, this is not a book about truth.

And if it were, who's to say what's true? As we have seen, even history books can be wrong.

If anything, this is a book about questions. And questions, you might say, are to the mind what lifeblood is to the vampire. Questions are the catalyst for curiosity, discovery and, ultimately, creation.

If Edison hadn't asked questions, you might be reading this by candlelight. If Edison hadn't asked questions, he would never have begun work on his communication device—for talking with the spirit world. (He died before completing it, rendering it unnecessary, I suppose.)

Why do I search out these stories?

Here honesty works as well as fabrication. To me it doesn't matter if the stories are true. If fact and fiction cohabit in the same chapter, that's okay too. After all, I'm a storyteller, not a journalist; I'm a collector, not a historian.

In fact, these are not even my stories. But I record them because they're important to me—important because of what they can do.

They can inspire curiosity, and curiosity is a golden link to the fantastic. And fantasy is as nourishing as sunlight.

These wonderful tales can be our ticket back to the days of childhood and wonder. They're our bridge to imagination, maybe to creation itself. They are a magical oasis in a science-centered desert that has no place for goblins and fairies and dragons in the lake.

And the words of these stories are magic words. They have the power to transform. I have seen them make an old man's eyes sparkle like the eyes of a child. I have seen a whole class of bored adolescents sit up and pay rapt attention. And I'll never forget an elderly woman who shook my hand and said, "You know, that reminds me of something odd that happened back when I was a little girl . . ."

Sure, I'll be the first to admit that ghosts aren't very good for the real estate business (I've talked to dozens of realtors; none will admit they know a reputedly haunted house). And monsters—especially lovable monsters like Champ—make Vermont seem even more like the theme park Northeast Kingdom poet and playwright David Budbill says it is in danger of becoming.

But still, year after year, the stories persist. And new ones come along.

Perhaps it all goes to show what each of us has known right along: There's a good deal more to Vermont than meets the eye.

The wild hills are before us,
where song and witchery lurk.

—H.P. Lovecraft
Vermont—A First Impression

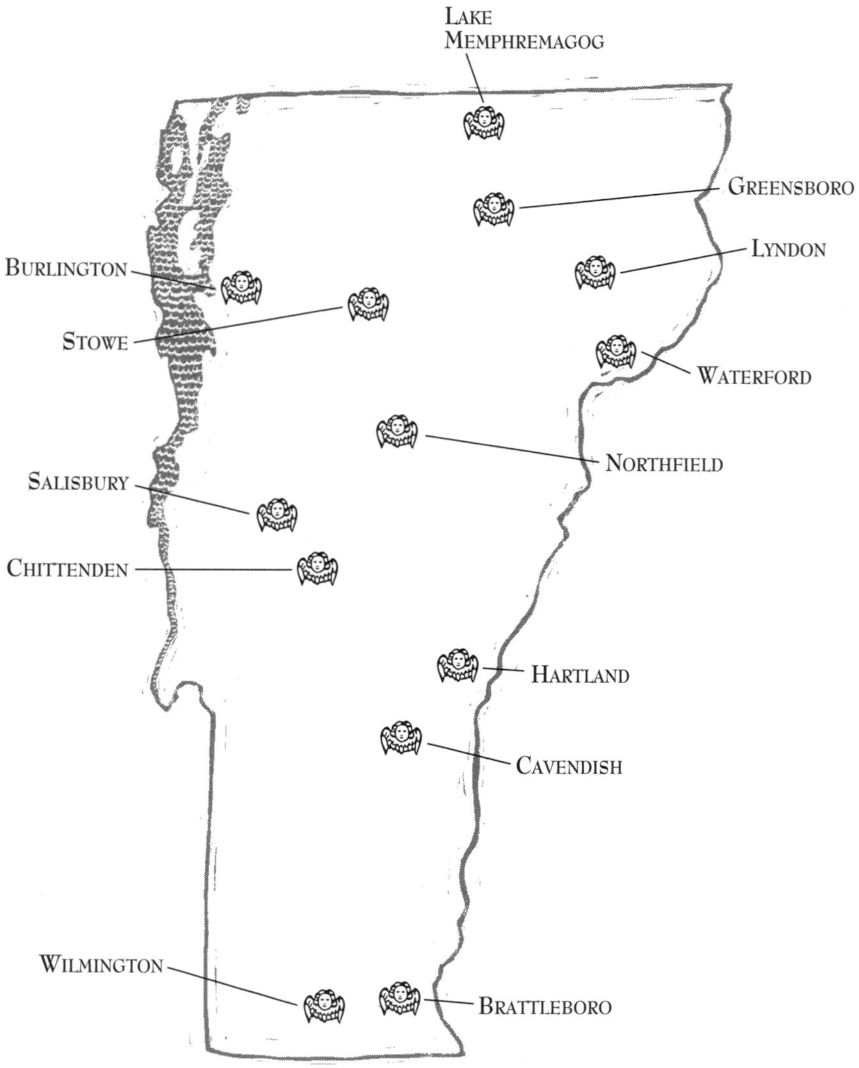

Lake Memphremagog

Greensboro

Lyndon

Burlington

Stowe

Waterford

Northfield

Salisbury

Chittenden

Hartland

Cavendish

Wilmington

Brattleboro

Vermont's Ghostly Gallery

I suspect every town in Vermont has at least one haunted house. And because we have 255 political divisions—237 towns, 9 cities, 2 unorganized towns, 3 unorganized townships and 4 gores—telling the story of each ghostly residence would require a work nothing short of encyclopedic.

Consequently, in the following pages, we'll only be able to visit a few of Vermont's more notable ghostly haunts.

The first section, *Communing with Spirits*, introduces Vermonters who have held conversations with mysterious supernatural entities. In one case, the dialogue cost the individual his reputation; in another case, it cost the man's life.

In the second division, we'll visit a few *Haunted Houses*, just to get a sampling of what can lurk behind closed doors.

And in the last section, as a reminder that ghosts don't confine their activities to houses, we'll explore a number of *Haunted Spots*—parcels of land whose ethereal boundaries natives and visitors cross at their own risk.

To begin our journey, we'll travel to Chittenden, a little mountain town not far from Rutland.

The story of the Eddy brothers is one of the weirdest things ever to happen in Vermont. See if you don't agree . . .

Most of us learned long ago that it's not a good idea to talk to strangers, and nothing could be stranger than the entities you'll meet in this section.

Communing with Spirits

At last he was reduced, like the newly bereft mothers who came to wail at one last vision of babies doubly torn from the body, to belief at once grudging and enthusiastic.

—Seth Steinzor
Echoes of the Eddys

Chittenden's Ghost Shop

It was a case of nineteenth-century ghostbusting. The year: 1874. The investigator: Henry Steel Olcott, on assignment from the *New York Daily Graphic.* The target: highly peculiar goings-on at a remote Vermont farmhouse in the tiny mountain town of Chittenden.

The house was a shunned place. Some locals called it "the ghost shop"; others swore it was "the abode of the devil." It was owned by William and Horatio Eddy, two middle-aged nearly illiterate brothers, and their sister, Mary.

Olcott, renowned for his rigorous investigations of corruption in military arsenals and naval shipyards after the Civil War, had been awarded the title of Colonel.

But it wasn't bandits in uniform the Colonel was after this time—it was supernatural creatures, ghosts and spectral phenomena of such magnitude as to be unrivaled before or since. The events at the Eddy farm were so powerful and strange that people came from all over the world to witness them. In some circles, Chittenden, Vermont, became known as "The Spirit Capital of the Universe."

Olcott's job was to determine whether William and Horatio were villains or visionaries, humbugs or heroes. If they were gifted clairvoyants, he would tell the world there was some validity to this "spiritualism" business. If they were ingenious charlatans, he'd expose them and let public contempt do its worst. In either event, Olcott was determined to be fair.

In his comprehensive book, *The History of Spiritualism*, Sir Arthur Conan Doyle describes the Colonel this way: "Olcott was not at that time identified with any psychic movement—indeed his mind was prejudiced against it, and he approached his task rather in the spirit of an 'exposer.' He was a man of clear brain and outstanding ability, with a high sense of honor . . . loyal to a fault, unselfish, and with that rare moral courage which will follow truth and accept results even when they oppose one's expectations and desires. He was no mystical dreamer but a very practical man of affairs. . . ."

Perhaps there was no better man for the job. But what about the mysterious Eddy brothers themselves? What type of men were they?

Sketchy records indicate they were descended from a long line of psychics. In Salem, their maternal grandmother four times removed had been sentenced to be hanged for witchcraft in 1692. She escaped with the help of friends.

Their grandmother had second sight; she'd often go into trances and converse with entities no one else could see.

Their mother, Julia Ann MacCoombs of Weston, Vermont, moved to the Chittenden farmhouse when she married Zephaniah Eddy in 1846. There she amazed and frightened the townspeople with predictions and visions. Her husband, an abusive, narrow-minded lout, discouraged further displays of her powers, convinced they were the work of The Evil One. After a while, Julia learned to hide her gifts.

But the unseen forces were impossible to conceal when the couple began having children. Inexplicable pounding resounded through the barren rooms of the ramshackle farmhouse. The parents and their visitors heard disembodied voices near the cribs. Sometimes the helpless infants were removed from their beds and transported elsewhere by unseen hands.

As the boys grew, occult forces strengthened to the point that spirits became visible. On several occasions, Zephaniah said he saw his sons playing with unfamiliar children, children that would vanish when he approached. Billy and Horatio couldn't go to school; their unobservable companions made it impossible. Loud hammering from nowhere disrupted the local one-room schoolhouse. There were tales of invisible hands yanking books away from terrified children. Objects—ink wells, chalk and rulers—were reported to fly around the room.

Zephaniah beat his sons, but the strange antics continued. He grew furious every time the boys fell spontaneously into a trance. First he'd accuse them of being slackers; then he'd declare they were in league with the devil. He'd try to wake them by punching or pinching them until their skin was black and blue. But the boys didn't waken.

Once, at the advice of a Christian friend, Anson Ladd, Zephaniah doused the boys with boiling water. When that indelicate approach failed, he allowed Ladd to drop a red-hot coal into William's hand to exorcise the devil. The boy didn't stir, but he bore a scar in his palm until his dying day.

Then, perhaps in a moment of twisted inspiration, Zephaniah realized he could profit from the "devil's" work. In exchange for a goodly sum of money, he released his sons to the custody of a traveling showman who took them on tour throughout the U.S., Canada and Europe.

They toured for fourteen years, performing their odd feats not only in front of audiences, but also before skeptics and self-proclaimed "psychic investigators" who tied them up to keep them from cheating, or filled their mouths with hot wax to prevent "ventriloquism." Punched, poked, prodded and pinched, they were left indelibly scarred and permanently misshapen—but their gifts were never discredited. The Eddys were mobbed in Lynn, Massachusetts, stoned in Danvers, even shot. William Eddy was irreparably disfigured by bullet wounds.

It is difficult to imagine a more horrible childhood. When the parents died, the brothers and Mary retreated to the family place in Chittenden. It is no wonder they grew into cold, suspicious, unfriendly men who, Olcott reported, ". . . make newcomers feel ill at ease and unwelcome."

Clearly, these were not glib and affable con men.

They were something else.

But what?

It is at this point in 1874 that Colonel Olcott's adventure begins. Picture Olcott arriving by train in Rutland during the height of August's heat. Imagine the bumpy, dusty, sweaty, seven-mile journey by stagecoach into a "grassy valley shut in by the slopes of the Green Mountains." Here, Olcott entered the "plain, dull, and uninteresting town" of Chittenden. From there, he made his way to "the ghost shop," Eddy's isolated two-and-a-half-story farmhouse on the road south toward East Pittsford.

And imagine meeting the Eddys for the first time. Somber, sinister and silent, they must have been an unnerving pair. Olcott wrote, "There is nothing about [them] to inspire confidence on first acquaintance. The brothers . . . are sensitive, distant, and curt to strangers . . . [They] look more like hard-working rough farmers than prophets or priests [with their] dark complexions, black hair and eyes, stiff joints, [and] clumsy carriage . . . ." They also spoke in a thick Vermont dialect, which often made them difficult to understand.

But in the ten weeks Colonel Olcott spent with the brothers, it wasn't horrors that he witnessed. Instead, it was a fantastic display of mind-numbing spiritual phenomena that even now remains without explanation.

Nowadays, we're not used to spiritualist displays. We wonder just exactly what Olcott saw in that 17-by-35.5-foot "circle room" above the kitchen of the Eddys' mysterious farmhouse.

Apparently the seances progressed something like this:

Every night of the week except Sunday, guests and visitors assembled on wooden benches before a platform lighted only by a kerosene lamp recessed in a barrel.

William Eddy, the primary medium, would mount the platform and enter a tiny closet known as his "spirit cabinet." For a suspenseful moment, all would be silent. Then far-off voices would speak or sing, often accompanied by music. Tambourines came to life and soared around the stage; ectoplasmic hands appeared, grappling, waving, touching the spectators.

Tension mounted.

Shortly, from behind the curtained door of the cabinet, ethereal forms began to emerge. One at a time or in groups. Twenty, even thirty in the course of an evening. Sometimes they were completely visible and seemingly solid. Other times they'd only partially materialize, or remain transparent. The figures varied in size from that of an infant to those well over six feet (William Eddy himself was only five-foot nine). Although the most familiar ghostly visitors were elderly Vermonters or American Indians (the sprightly Honto in her beads and moccasins or the sullen giant Santum) a vast array of representative nationalities appeared in costume: black Africans, Russians, Kurds, Orientals and more.

Where'd they all come from? Olcott was well versed in the methods of stage magicians and fraudulent mediums. His detailed examinations of the spirit cabinet disclosed only plaster and lathe. No trap doors, no hidden compartments, no room for anyone but the medium himself.

Then the apparitions would perform, singing, dancing, chatting with the spectators; they'd produce weapons, scarves and musical instruments. In fact, the wondrous Eddy exhibitions included all the manifestations known to psychic science at the time: rappings, moving objects, spirit paintings and drawings, prophesy, speaking in strange tongues, healing, spirit communication, human levitation, musical instruments playing, uncanny hands appearing, ghostly writing, remote vision, clairvoyance.

But most amazing were the materializations. Olcott concluded that such a show would require a whole troupe of actors and several trunks full of costumes. With the help of carpenters and engineers, Olcott made a thorough search of the premises. His conclusion: there was simply no place to hide people or props.

And such a show would be expensive to put on every night. The brothers were poor; they, along with their sister, did all the housework themselves. Half the visitors didn't pay, the rest gave only eight dollars a week for room and board. No charge was ever made for the seances. So how could the Eddys compensate actors, researchers, costumers and the designers of complicated "illusions"?

Some of the spectators recognized friends and long-deceased relatives among the apparitions. One woman spoke at length, in Russian, to the specter of her dead husband. How was it possible? The illiterate Eddys hadn't really mastered their own tongue, how could they hold fluent conversations in no fewer than six foreign languages?

As part of his investigation, Olcott got the Honto spirit to agree to be weighed on a Fairbanks platform scale he'd brought along for the purpose. She appeared to be about five-three and, if corporeal, would weigh around 135 pounds. She was weighed four times on the same evening. The results were puzzling: 88, 58, 58 and 65 pounds. William Eddy himself weighed 179 pounds.

At the end of the demonstration, the forms would either reenter the cabinet or vanish into mist before the wide eyes of puzzled observers.

One account was told by an eyewitness—Franklin Bolles of Hartford, Connecticut—in a letter to the *Rutland Herald* dated June 1875: ". . . my wife's mother . . . deceased March 1859, at the age of 78 years, appeared to us in white clothing, looking so natural that we recognized her instantly. She stood outside the cabinet curtain, leaned her body forward, and stretched out her arms to her daughter, as if she were longing to embrace her. Mrs. Prior asked if she could not speak to us, and she seemed to make a desperate effort to comply. But suddenly, as if she had exhausted all her power of materialization in the attempt, her arms dropped, and her form melted down to the floor, and disappeared from our view. The figure did not dissolve into a mist and disperse laterally, but sank down and disappeared, as if every particle comprising her frame had suddenly lost its cohesion with every other, and the whole fell into a heap together."

One investigator, Dr. Beard, a medical man from New York, attracted a lot of attention when, on the strength of a single visit, he proclaimed that the figures were all nothing but impersonations by William Eddy himself. Beard boasted that he could easily reproduce all the effects with "three dollars worth of theatrical properties."

Olcott's longer and more rigorous investigation suggests something far more complicated. So does sworn testimony by numerous witnesses. One example comes from a Doctor Hodges of Stoneham, Massachusetts, who, along with four other witnesses, signed a docu-

6

ment saying: "We certify . . . that Santum was out on the platform when another Indian of almost as great a stature came out, and the two passed and repassed each other as they walked up and down. At the same time, a conversation was being carried on between [spirits known as] George Dix, Mayflower, old Mrs. Morse and Mrs. Eaton inside the cabinet. We recognized the familiar voice of each."

One wonders how William alone could have pulled that off.

Olcott's ten-week stay at the farmhouse seems a tremendous feat of endurance considering the plain food, hard living and unfriendly hosts. He came away disliking the gloomy brothers. Yet at the same time, Olcott was absolutely confident of their psychic powers. He chronicled his experience in a series of articles for the *New York Daily Graphic* and in a remarkable book called *People from the Other World.* Reading these today, it is difficult to imagine any precaution this fair-minded researcher didn't take. The book is full of detailed drawings of the house and its construction, all of which illustrate the measures Olcott took to investigate and disclose deception. He also reproduces statements from respectable carpenters and tradespeople who examined everything for trickery.

In all, Olcott chronicled the appearance of well over 400 different supernatural entities. He collected hundreds of witness testimonies and dozens of sworn affidavits from laborers, lawyers, farmers, physicians, merchants, musicians, bankers, bakers, housewives and historians. All had personally observed the manifestations of men, women, children and even babies, most of which came from the spirit cabinet, then roamed freely around the "circle room."

Whenever a seance ended, the spirit cabinet and William were thoroughly searched. Both showed the same result: a chair with a man tied to it—and nothing else. No Indian buckskins, no costumes or clothing, no musical instruments, spears, daggers or pistols—just a man in a deep trance.

Horatio Eddy died in 1922. William followed in 1932 at age 99. Now, unfortunately, so much time has passed that very few, if anyone, can remember the intriguing brothers.

In 1944, Alton Blackington interviewed several Chittenden residents for a radio show about the Eddys. One man recalled a visit to William and Horatio. He found them working alone in a cornfield. After a few minutes, ". . . two other figures appeared out of nowhere and followed the Eddys wherever they went."

As recently as 1980, Burlington journalist Greg Guma interviewed two elderly Chittenden residents who had known the family.

Mabel Potter, aged 80 at the time of the interview, had moved into Horatio's house in 1924. She recalled how townspeople had perceived the Eddys: ". . . people here were scared to death of them. They thought they were witches, I guess. When we come up here, they spoke about them and everybody seemed to be awfully afraid of them."

Guma asked Mrs. Potter if she thought the Eddys were tricksters.

". . . I don't know. I think a lot of it was genuine because they'd been all over that house to find out about cupboards or closets that they could use to be doing something tricky."

On the other hand, Agnes Gould didn't believe any of it. Ninety-six years old when Guma interviewed her, she told how the family feuded and eventually split up as the popularity of theatrical spiritualism started to decline. "They'd get jealous of each other's power, each other's success," Mrs. Gould explained. "If they'd kept honor among themselves, they would have been the richest people in the world. They had people coming from all over the world."

Sister Mary Eddy moved to East Pittsford where she gave seances of her own. Horatio moved into a red house nearby, leaving William alone. When William died, he took the solution to the Eddy mystery with him to the grave. Since then, as far as we know, he's held his silence.

So what are we to make of this today, almost a century and a quarter after the fact? Explanations run from the mundane to the arcane.

If the events at the Eddy farm were not a hoax, then something very strange and wonderful happened there.

But what? Were the myriad apparitions actually the spirits of the dead?

Olcott's documentation—corroborated by much sworn testimony

and the conclusions of a second investigative reporter sent by another New York newspaper—argues against a hoax. Though thoroughly skeptical and relentlessly analytical, Olcott came away believing that the Eddys were communing with spirits.

But if the dead don't return, then what were those incredible creatures? Could they have been some extroverted ectoplasmic extension of the sullen, sleeping William? Did he, through some biological process yet unknown, produce the visions from his mind or the matter of his body?

Or could the creatures have been something else, something stranger, like elemental pranksters posing as departed loved ones, motivated by forces, drives and desires we cannot even guess at?

The theatrical quality of the demonstrations suggests that someone—or something—was putting on a show.

Madam Helena Blavatsky, whom Olcott met at Chittenden, had a chilling explanation that hints at sinister purpose. Though she didn't believe spirits of the dead returned to earth, she believed nonhuman spirits existed, spirits who could, on occasion, interact with mankind.

She postulated that the Eddys, unwittingly, had given such spirits a point of entry into our world. Trying to develop contacts with the dead, she explained, "only opens the door to a swarm of 'spooks,' good, bad or indifferent, to which the medium becomes a slave for life." She warned that these and similar experiments could interfere with the evolution of human souls, for some spirits "are most dangerous."

Could cunning, malevolent spirits have been putting on a show to divert people's attention from more constructive spiritual development? Maybe. There is no doubt that this whole country—indeed the entire Western world—was "distracted" by spiritualism for several decades. There were never any definitive conclusions, of course. And as a fad, spiritualism's popularity had pretty much faded by the time of William Eddy's death in 1932.

Wherever the truth lies, the Eddy visions so influenced Olcott that he came away a changed man, a believer. Later, along with Madam Blavatsky, Olcott co-founded the Theosophical Society, whose membership included Thomas Edison, W. B. Yeats, Nehru, Piet Mondrian and many others. The Society still exists, but doesn't have the following it once enjoyed. Perhaps today those same malevolent spirits are still around. And perhaps they're still distracting us, but in a very different way.

What the Dickens?

IN 1870, LITERARY SUPERSTAR CHARLES DICKENS was in England busily at work on his new novel, *The Mystery of Edwin Drood*. It was being released in installments, a chapter at a time. When Dickens last left off, Drood was missing, maybe dead. Thousands of British and American readers were eager to see what would happen next. They would never find out, for on June 9, 1870 Charles Dickens died, and the solution to the Drood mystery died with him.

Imagine the disappointment of Dickens's fans.

Now—although it may be a bit more taxing—imagine yourself as the spirit of Charles Dickens waking up on another plane, in the so-called spirit world. You're dead, but you still feel responsible to your loyal readers. What, if anything, can you do?

Some people believe Dickens went on a three-year search to find a spirit medium who was *in harmony* with him.

1872: the heyday of spiritualism. In a boarding house on Oak Street in Brattleboro, Thomas Power James, a 30-year-old printer, was invited to attend a seance in his landlady's parlor.

A contemporary newspaper account describes James as a good-looking, dark-haired man with a mustache and slate-gray eyes. He was intelligent but poorly educated, having finished only about five years of school. He claimed to know nothing of spiritualism until his friends dragged him off to the landlady's seance.

Seated in the Victorian parlor, James went spontaneously into a trance. Then, as if possessed, he wrote a message for one of the other sitters. The note was from a dead girl to her father.

Perhaps it was at that moment the questing spirit of Charles Dickens went drifting through Brattleboro, Vermont. Perhaps he noticed the automatic writing and concluded that James was a powerful medium. "Ah-ha!" Dickens might have said, "Mr. James is precisely the gentleman I've been looking for."

Still in his trance, James wrote out another automatic message, this one addressed to himself. The controlling spirit requested a private interview—just James and the spirit—on November 15. It was signed "Charles Dickens."

During this "private seance" Dickens asked James for help: together they would complete *The Mystery of Edwin Drood*. Their effort would commence on Christmas Eve, Dickens's favorite night.

Although Dickens promised "some pecuniary benefit," James showed little confidence in the odd collaboration. Then the process started to get results.

Night after night, James sat alone at his desk with two sharpened pencils and a stack of paper torn into half sheets. He'd slip into a trance and begin to write. Clearly the handwriting was not like his own. At first it was neat and precise, but as the fury of creation continued, it became large, careless, nearly incoherent.

Communication was impaired by stormy weather. If atmospheric conditions were bad, James's trance would last only a few minutes. On a good day, the ethereal partnership could labor for ten to fifteen hours.

The text of the manuscript was often accompanied by encouraging notes from Dickens to James, saying things like, "We are doing finely. I am more than satisfied with the result of this undertaking."

It seems that Dickens had high hopes for the collaboration. He wrote, "When this work is finished, you will continue to be my amanuensis. I shall write more after this." He said his new work was to be called *The Life and Adventures of Bockley Wickleheap*.

At the end of a session, James would awaken with unnumbered pages strewn all around him. He would remember nothing, except for the occasional vision of Dickens sitting beside him. It was always the spirit who terminated the sessions by placing a hand on the medium's shoulder; a hand, James said, "as cold and heavy as the hand of death."

In spite of the publicity James received for his efforts, many contemporary accounts were not favorable. The Boston *Traveller* portrayed James as a wandering malcontent, a failed businessman and a generally sleazy character, "full of whims and unaccountable impulses." Significantly, they also disclosed one instance of James being involved in literary plagiarism. He "was writing a new play by the title of *Euphrasia*, but some of the favored few to whom portions were read were somewhat surprised to find it taken, almost word for word, from an old play, *The Grecian Daughter*."

The *Telegraph* of Nashua, New Hampshire, had once employed James. They, too, raised questions about his character based on firsthand experience. Yet they generously added, "Still we must give him credit for considerable ingenuity, as the imposition he has attempted is one of the cleverest in conception and execution in modern times."

The Mystery of Edwin Drood by Charles Dickens and Thomas Power James was eventually published on October 25, 1873—just in time for Christmas. In spite of the controversy, it made little impact on the local or national press. Critics were in disagreement not only about the medium's character, but also the spirit's.

Yes, the spelling was English, the diction was Dickensian, and the style was distinctly non-American, but experts said it just wasn't Dickens.

Perhaps Conan Doyle summed it up best in his book *The Edge of the Unknown:*

"No one who reads it can deny that it is an excellent imitation of the great author's style, but the most unconvincing part was the narrative itself, which was clumsy and improbable. . . . No one with any critical faculty would say that the result was an entirely unworthy one, though if written by the living Dickens it would certainly not have improved his reputation. It reads . . . like Dickens gone flat."

James vanished from the literary scene. Apparently Dickens went with him because *The Life and Adventures of Bockley Wickleheap* has never appeared. And *The Mystery of Edwin Drood* is also the mystery of Thomas Power James.

If the spirit of Charles Dickens had actually come here to finish *Edwin Drood*, we can easily understand: over the years many authors have been attracted to Vermont. But for a writer with so much insight into characterization, "Old Boz" might have been expected to choose a more credible collaborator.

Sam Connor of Cavendish

IN THE WORLDS OF FOLKLORE AND OCCULT LITERATURE, stories of people seeing other people's ghosts are legion. But the town of Cavendish one-ups them all with a most extraordinary tale.

Long ago—sometime early in the last century—a Vermonter named Sam Connor told his friends about the strangest adventure of his life. Once, while crossing a local swamp at night, he suddenly became aware that he wasn't alone.

He looked around in the gloom, his heart pounding.

Then he saw it! Someone was coming toward him through the eerie marshland.

Connor didn't break stride and neither did the stranger. As the other traveler got closer, Connor couldn't believe what he was seeing. Why, it was absolutely impossible!

Later, he told his friends what had happened. The sensation, he said, was exactly like ". . . when a man walks towards a long mirror and sees his image coming with equal pace to meet him at the glass."

What Sam Connor saw was his own double!

When the two were close enough, the look-alike paused and spoke to the dumfounded Connor. But this was no idle conversation between two weary travelers. The double got right to the point; he warned that one year from that very day, Sam Connor would die. Some of Sam's friends believed the story, some didn't, but as the fatal date grew closer, Sam Connor found the deadly prediction impossible to ignore.

Then, all too soon, the dreaded day arrived.

To get his mind off things, Connor joined a group of his neighbors at a barn-raising. Since everyone was aware of the grim prophesy, Connor wasn't permitted to participate in the more dangerous tasks, like climbing to high places, positioning heavy timbers or getting too near the saws and axes.

Toward the end of the afternoon, the group broke for supper. Everyone washed and headed for the farmhouse, talking and laughing good-naturedly.

Lagging behind, Connor noticed a brace that needed securing. It would be an easy, quick job—there was nothing dangerous about it. And, by God, he was man enough to take care of it, Fate be damned!

After carefully placing a ladder against the skeletal frame of the barn, Connor climbed up to fix the brace. No problem, just a few swings of the hammer and he'd join his friends at the supper table.

Balanced and holding on tightly, Connor deftly pounded the wooden dowel into place.

In the distance, the cheerful sounds of his friends at dinner made him want to hurry, but he resisted. No doubt he was imagining the hearty farm fare: fried chicken, squash with maple syrup, biscuits and freshly baked apple pie. Why, he could almost taste it.

But it wasn't to be. No one knows exactly what happened or why it happened. Perhaps Connor shifted his weight. Perhaps he ducked to avoid the sting of a wasp. Perhaps he was bumped by a sudden gust of wind. In any event, the ladder slid against the beam. By reflex he dropped the hammer, grabbing for the frame of the barn. His sudden motion propelled the ladder out from under him. It crashed against the wooden floor like the deadly report of a rifle.

Connor hung from the beam for a few seconds. As he groped for a tighter hold, slivers from the rough-hewn timber bit at his calloused hands.

He cried for help, but no one was close enough to hear.

Whether seconds passed or long minutes, no one can say. All we know is that Sam Connor fell to his death while his friends feasted nearby.

It was exactly one year since the uncanny confrontation with his ghostly double in the depths of that mysterious Cavendish swamp.

HAUNTED HOUSES

ALMOST EVERY WEEK, I get cards or calls telling me about haunted houses I'd never heard about before. I never realized there are so many! It is as if Vermont has two populations: one living, the other dead. I'm beginning to wonder which has the greater number . . .

Wilmington's White House

WILMINGTON IS SITUATED on southern Vermont's spine, about halfway between Brattleboro and Bennington. Along Route 9, on a hill less than a mile east of town, there's a magnificent turn-of-the-century mansion called The White House. Ancient trees grace the yard, providing shade for immense Victorian porches upstairs and down. There's something elegant about the place, something tranquil. Admiring it from outside, nothing hints that strange phenomena have been recorded within.

In 1915, Vermont lumber baron Martin Brown and his wife, Clara, had the place constructed. Clara quickly came to love her beautiful twenty-nine-room estate with its mahogany walls, winding staircase and eight fireplaces. She took great pride in decorating it herself, leaving the mark of her personality on every room.

Clara ordered custom-designed furniture and commissioned made-to-order wall coverings from France. Lengths of deep rose carpeting lined the halls. With unrelenting care, she personally oversaw everything, lavishing much love on each tasteful detail.

Perhaps in a moment of whimsy, the Browns installed a secret passageway. Even today one can vanish through an opening behind a downstairs cabinet, ascend a hidden staircase, then magically reappear in an upstairs closet.

The Browns lived in The White House for nearly fifty years. Then, in 1962, Martin Brown died. Family and friends assumed the 85-year-old Clara would sell the place and move to more manageable quarters.

"Sell?" said Clara. "I'm going to live here the rest of my life."

And true to her word, the determined old woman lived on the estate for another ten years. In 1972, she died quietly of a stroke.

But life . . . life of some sort . . . seemed to continue in The White House. Noises, creaks, rumbles. Sure, such things occur in any old building, but here there was something more.

Today, The White House has been reincarnated as an outstanding country inn. And—if you can believe the stories—some of those who stay there may be travelers from another realm.

Doors open and close seemingly of their own will. Air moves in closed rooms. Unnatural sounds can be heard . . .

And there have been other incidents.

One of the chambermaids reported that she frequently heard someone calling her name, but when she looked, no one was there.

Even the doubting innkeeper, Robert Grinold, admits to a peculiar puzzle. "There is always a cold draft in this one particular area [of the kitchen]. I have driven myself crazy trying to find the source of that draft."

Jan Shields, a writer visiting the house, experienced the same phenomenon but described it differently: it was not so much a draft, Sheilds said, as it was a penetrating chill.

Who, or what, could be responsible?

Was the deceased Clara Brown guilty of understatement when she said she would live there for the rest of her life? Is it possible that she's living there still?

Much of the ghost's activity seems to be around room number nine. It was never Clara Brown's bedroom, but it still contains many of her treasured belongings.

One morning, a guest—also named Brown—reported a puzzling incident. "I was awakened [last night] by this white-haired woman sitting in the chair near my bed. [The old woman] said, 'You know, my dear, I don't mind your staying here, but one Mrs. Brown in this room is quite enough.'"

Another incident involved a college student named Kelly who worked for the inn one summer as a chambermaid. Kelly was making up the bed in room nine when all of a sudden the doors on either side of the fireplace began opening and closing, one after the other. The frightened young woman swore there was no wind or anything else that could cause such a disturbance.

So what did this supernatural display mean?

Perhaps it was Clara Brown repeating her message—one Mrs. Brown in this room is quite enough—for the frightened chambermaid's full name was Kelly Brown.

The Spirit's Spirits

Few people driving through Lyndon fail to notice the Cahoon House on the Red Village Road. In fact, people have been noticing it for years because it's the oldest Lyndon homestead.

But this story doesn't begin in Vermont. It begins in Providence, Rhode Island, in the late 1700s. There, a merchant named Daniel Cahoon owned a potato-whiskey distillery and an import-export company. For a while, his enterprises were prosperous. But then the Revolutionary War, coupled with relentless taxation, drove him out of business.

Hoping for a new start, Cahoon moved to northeastern Vermont. There, along with a committee of other New Englanders, he settled in Lyndon.

Cahoon quickly established a sawmill and a gristmill. He built a grand new house—the first in town with two stories. His taste for "spirits" led him to have a wine cellar built into the foundation of his new home.

Cahoon's many contributions to the town earned him the affection and respect of almost everyone. Sooner or later, he, or one of his sons, held just about every public office in Lyndon: judge, town clerk, lister, selectman, even legislator. As was the custom of the day, he conducted public business from an in-home office. He also opened his home to special community events, including weddings and parties.

But tragedy struck on September 13, 1811. The heroic 74-year-old Daniel Cahoon rushed into his pasture to save a child from a charging bull. The child survived, but Cahoon was gored to death.

Believing her husband should have been able to elude the rampaging beast, Mrs. Cahoon blamed the incident on Daniel's taste for spirits. In response, she had his much-loved wine cellar walled-up before "any others in my family are destroyed by it."

Lyndon pioneer Daniel Cahoon died at the beginning of the nineteenth century, but there seems to be some question about whether he moved on to become a settler in the next realm. There is much evidence to suggest he never left his wonderful old house.

Daniel's descendants kept the house in the family for nearly two centuries. During the 1960s, Clayton Hoffman and his wife, Hortense, gave educational tours of the premises. They often told about Daniel's ghost as wide-eyed school children, college students or tourists peered nervously into the building's dark corners.

Mrs. Hoffman liked to tell about her first encounter with her husband's great-great-great grandfather. It was about three o'clock in the middle of a freezing winter night. The slam of the front door woke her up. Then she heard feet stomping on wooden floorboards below, followed by a loud commotion that filled the downstairs hall.

In the morning, she asked her husband what he'd been up to.

Clayton assured her he had no idea what had happened—he'd been fast asleep. What she'd heard was Daniel, the family ghost.

After that, Mrs. Hoffman lost a lot of sleep to the sounds of heavy breathing, boot-stomping and stair-climbing. Most of the noise came from what the family called "the haunted chamber," the room where Daniel's corpse had been laid out before burial.

But after his death, Daniel Cahoon remained every bit as congenial and hospitable as he had been in life. He especially liked to entertain house guests. His mood always seemed festive, if a little mischievous.

One visitor recalled sitting on her bed fixing her hair before turning in. She was startled when the mattress beside her suddenly pressed down as if some unseen weight had settled there.

Another guest was awakened as the bedcovers slipped from her shoulders. She checked to see if her husband was stealing the blankets. But no. The blankets were being pulled from the other direction. And whatever was tugging on them was invisible.

One guest's sleep was eerily disturbed by the sound of music. The radio was definitely off. Everyone else was sleeping. Yet, somehow, the music seemed to get louder and louder. The guest recognized the strains of chamber music, the kind that was popular in the late 1700s. Then indistinct voices began murmuring. The voices were joined by the sounds of silver and glassware tinkling. Feminine laughter rang within the walls. Yet the guest—checking once more to be sure—was absolutely alone in the room as the odor of tobacco filled the air.

No one knows why spirits linger so long after their remains have returned to the dust. Daniel Cahoon's descendants believe his motives are fairly straightforward: they say he's searching for that wine cellar his wife had walled up some two hundred years before.

Vermont's Educated Spirits

We often hear the familiar refrain: Educated people don't believe in ghosts. But apparently ghosts believe in education, especially higher education. Or so it would seem from the number of spirits in residence at Vermont colleges. As I researched this book, I came to believe that every college in Vermont has enrolled at least one ghost. The single exception might be Community College of Vermont, but only because it doesn't have a campus.

There are ghostly theatergoers at Castleton State College and St. Michael's College. Plainfield's Goddard College has a building with a haunted upstairs corridor where someone, or something, paces late at night. The Henry Prescott Chaplin Memorial Library at Norwich University has been haunted for years. Director of Libraries Paul Heller says, "People have said books suddenly pop off the shelves, lights flip on and off. And students walking near the library late at night claim to have glanced through the windows to see what might be a man striding past the red 'exit' signs in nineteenth-century dress." Though the library has recently been converted to classrooms, the ghost is apparently still there.

In terms of sheer quantity of haunted buildings, the University of Vermont in Burlington gets the prize. Ghostly goings-on have been reported in at least seven buildings.

Converse Hall is a big, brooding, gothic-looking structure that sits like Frankenstein's castle near the Medical Center Hospital of Vermont. In the 1920s, a lonely and overworked medical student named Henry supposedly hanged himself in the attic. Apparently he's dead but not gone. Since then, strange things have happened in the rooms and corridors of Converse. Doors mysteriously open and shut. Water faucets turn on. Typewriters operate without typists. Bewildered students discover their rooms have been rearranged. A certain rocking chair is seen to rock . . . all by itself. One story involves a group of students preparing for a party. One of them joked, "Hey Henry, why don't you join us tonight?" At just that moment, the light in the room flickered as if to say Henry would be there.

South Prospect Street boasts several haunted buildings.

Number 322, the Continuing Education building, seems to house a number of active spirits. I spoke with one woman who recalled disturbances such as pounding, flickering electrical lights and computers switching off and on without benefit of a human hand on the switch. She said when the floor started vibrating, she knew it was time to get out!

Number 194, the UVM Admissions Building, is the site of a similar haunting. The signs are comparable: footsteps when no one's around, doors opening and closing, noises from nowhere. This haunting, like Converse Hall's, is attributed to a suicide: someone supposedly shot himself in one of the upstairs rooms around the turn of the century. In an unsettling encounter, a UVM security guard reported that he'd felt something invisible moving by him on the stairs.

Nearby, South Williams Street is another ghostly ghetto.

The Public Relations office (86 South Williams Street) was once owned by a Dr. Booth who, apparently, still keeps office hours inside. There are tales of noises, flickering lights and weird air currents that make it difficult to open certain doors. In fact, anything strange happening in the building is routinely blamed on Dr. Booth's ghost. Admittedly, the good doctor's spirit has never been very spirited, but some of UVM's ghosts are a little more aggressive. Spirits have not only been sensed and heard . . . but seen.

The Counseling and Testing Center is in an old brick mansion on the corner of South Williams and Main. It is said that people in this building never feel alone, even when they're by themselves.

For example, in the mid-'70s, head secretary Louise Gulla was working alone on Saturday. Around four in the afternoon, she heard the front door open and close. She expected a colleague to step in and say hello. But no one arrived. Then she heard footsteps going up the stairs. She listened as if for the other shoe to drop, but no one ever came back down.

Later, when a student dropped by, Gulla asked him to go upstairs and see who was there. The student checked thoroughly and, needless to say, found no one.

Another story involves the janitor who was mopping floors in the dark early-morning hours. Something unseen knocked his bucket over, making quite a mess. When the janitor looked around to see what was happening, the lights flashed on and off. He actually saw the light switch on the wall flipping up and down by itself.

The janitor put in for a transfer. And got it.

But the experiences in this especially haunted building get even more dramatic.

One of its directors—a psychologist and presumably a rational man—reports sitting alone in his office one night when he saw what he described as "a spectral image gliding down the stairway."

He observed it quite clearly; it was ". . . an elderly man with distinct facial features and a bulbous nose—but [he was] kind of translucent and shimmering like a jellyfish."

Before drifting away, the specter glowered at the professor as if to ask, What are you doing here, mister?

The professor asked himself the same question and left.

Other people working alone in the building have heard the usual sounds of a ghost: footsteps, doors and the like. But this building offers other sounds as well: sneezing and coughing, as if the spirit world is not free of ghostly germs and viruses.

No one knows for sure whose ghost haunts the Counseling and Testing Center. Most think it's the spirit of Captain Jacobs, who owned the house a century ago. He died, so the story goes, of an upper respiratory infection. And he still has the cough to prove it.

Directly across Main Street from the Counseling and Testing Center is the Alumni Relations office, an elegant yellow brick two-story building known as Grassemount. I spoke with Lynne Ballard who worked there when Grassemount housed UVM's Continuing Education Department. She and several colleagues often experienced benign ghostly antics. She recalls one evening when she was working late. Between 11:00 and midnight, her concentration was suddenly disturbed by loud noises upstairs: doors slamming, drawers banging, pounding footsteps. Fearing vandals or thieves—but suspecting the ghost—she phoned her husband, Bill, who was overseer of campus security. Though skeptical about ghostly noisemakers, Lynne's no-nonsense husband arrived to find the commotion so active, loud and unsettling that he quickly summoned security guards. The officers arrived, searched and left, finding nothing and leaving Bill embarrassed but far less skeptical.

UVM is known as an equal opportunity employer, at least in the ghost department.

On the corner of South Prospect and Main Streets, there is a house, built in 1809, called the Bittersweet. Its name comes from the vines growing there. The Bittersweet houses the University of Vermont's environmental programs.

One wintry night in 1984, an administrative assistant named Madonna Gordon and her 15-year-old daughter, Tish, were passing the house. They saw a light in an upstairs window. Worried there might be an ailing colleague inside, Madonna and her daughter went in to investigate.

Madonna called out as they made their way down the shadowy hall. All of a sudden, they stopped in their tracks. Someone was standing at the end of the hall! Someone unfamiliar. A woman, about 40, with odd, upswept hair. Her clothing looked strange, too: she wore a long bell-shaped skirt and a high-collared blouse—the style worn around 1900.

Tish later described the apparition this way: "It was like a shadow of a person, but it was a three-dimensional shadow . . ."

Madonna saw the apparition several more times, but never again as clearly. Occasionally, UVM security guards report seeing a gray, filmy shape. Others report the routine symptoms of a haunting: doors opening and closing, lights going on and off, footsteps when nobody's around.

The Bittersweet's ghost has never identified herself. Some theorize she's the spirit of Margaret L.H. Smith who lived there from the 1930s to the 1950s. Mrs. Smith died at 94, blind, poor and without family. Her twilight years were sad largely due to the loneliness she suffered after the tragic death of her husband. Her sadness may live on.

Shard Villa

No one could pass Shard Villa in Salisbury without thinking, *That house just has to be haunted.* With its Italianate-Gothic-Second-Empire hodgepodge of Victorian architecture and its on-site mausoleum, it looks totally out of place in the Vermont landscape.

Quite obviously, Shard Villa is the product of a mind with a flair for the dramatic.

Its builder, a lawyer named Columbus Smith, made his fortune by selling or reclaiming European estates for clients who'd relocated to the United States. Shard Villa was constructed with money that Smith made arguing Mary Francis Shard's holdings out of the hands of the English Crown. Legal proceedings took fourteen years and required six voyages to England. Supposedly Smith argued for forty days, during which his hair and beard turned white.

When he returned to Vermont in 1872, he began building his mansion. Shard Villa has three stories with thirty rooms full of frescoes and statuary. It's dark, somber and imposing, an ideal setting for an Alfred Hitchcock thriller. Or a ghost story.

It was within its cold limestone walls that Smith's life turned from success to tragedy. His son, William, died at 14, victim of a neurological infection. A stone bears the melancholy inscription: "1881, June 13, Willie died." Salisbury historian Max Peterson relates, "The loss of his only son resulted in Columbus's physical and mental decline . . ."

Perhaps the death of his daughter, Mary Elizabeth, sixteen years later finished him off. His health deteriorated to the point that he had to be confined to a wheelchair.

Irving Bacheller, the children's tutor, recalled, "On one of my last visits to Shard Villa, its master had lost his health and reason. At night, I was awakened by a curious animal roar from the lips of the stricken man—[a] weird and melancholy sound ringing through the great house in which I had heard the merry laughter of children."

Today, some of that high strangeness remains. Though Columbus, his wife and their children are interred in the mausoleum on the premises, the Smiths may not be at rest.

At present—as was directed in Columbus's will—Shard Villa is being used as a home for the elderly. And, as if the old place were a bridge from this world to the next, otherworldly events regularly occur.

Jean Seeley, a former director, has claimed to have seen Columbus Smith walking the halls at night. A housekeeper swore the old man's ghost was in his bedroom whenever she went in to clean. Another employee saw flashes of light and a convergence of strange shadows.

Doors and windows mysteriously open and close. And things vanish in the house. A knife disappeared from a countertop next to the cook who was using it. One earring vanished from a set only to reappear later in another spot.

Cathy Blaise tells of an unusual happening in the second-floor library. "I was sitting upstairs reading and this cold enveloped me. I couldn't move."

Director Peggy Rocque was no believer in ghosts before she moved into Shard Villa. She brought her dog who never strayed from her side. But once in the house, it wouldn't follow her up the stairs. It would just stand at the bottom and whine. Later, Rocque had experiences of her own. Lying in bed at night, she would hear glass shattering.

But she never found anything broken. She also heard the piano playing downstairs, but every time she investigated, no one was at the keyboard. Once she discovered that the tub in an unused upstairs bathroom had been filled. This was especially odd because no one had ever been able to turn the rusty faucet!

Perhaps her eeriest experience was hearing a baby crying. Most of the staff heard it too—yet no baby could be found. In fact, no one could tell where the cries were coming from.

As far as I know, nothing truly terrifying has ever happened at Shard Villa. The presence seems somewhat playful, as if it's toying with people's minds and having some odd kind of fun.

And no one has been able to say if one ghost or many haunt Shard Villa's shadowy halls. The identity of the ghost or ghosts remains a mystery. Columbus Smith? Family member? Employee? Maybe one of the residents of the community-care home? The crying baby seems especially strange because there's no record of a baby ever dying there.

Some people have suggested the director try to contact the ghost through a medium or recruit an exorcist to evict the spectral tenants. So far, no director has wanted to do that. As Peggy Rocque says, "I'm . . . comfortable living with it the way it is. I don't want to stir something up that would make me uncomfortable to live here."

The Trembling House

ARTIST, WRITER AND INTERNATIONAL GHOST HUNTER James Reynolds tells of an odd experience he had while visiting Vermont. Back in the 1940s, as he was driving from Waterford to St. Johnsbury, he stopped to admire and sketch an ancient apple orchard.

But something wrenched his attention from the gnarled and twisted trees. Nearby, a small grove of maples nearly concealed an abandoned house. It was a plain two-story clapboard building with an attached woodshed. He describes it as needing paint so badly that it appeared almost silver. But there was something else . . . It may have been an optical illusion, a fantasy of light and shadow, but Reynolds was convinced the house was moving, actually shaking on its brick foundation as if caught in a minor earthquake. Stranger still, it shook in utter silence, without the slightest screech of straining timbers or rattling shutters.

Feeling a twitch of fear, Reynolds started back to his car. But he saw something else. A woman—dressed in a long dark wrapper and standing still as death—just staring at the house.

Her jaw was set, her eyes burned in their sockets. Reynolds swears they were angry eyes, filled with the essence of hatred. Then, as he watched her, the woman seemed to step back into the shadows and disappear.

Later, plagued by curiosity, Reynolds sought out a retired Waterford postmaster. Though Reynolds declines to identify his informant, he says the man had known Waterford firsthand since the turn of the century and long before that from the stories of his father and grandfather. He was able to tell Reynolds the full story of the trembling house and the specter that watched it.

A man named Sheller had built the place around 1880 as a rental property. His tenant was Jake Farr of Woodstock. Shortly after Jake moved in, he found himself a wife—Sally. Sally was a beautiful woman with dark hair and haunting eyes. She could handle an ax or a gun, but she left that kind of thing to Jake. Instead, she busied herself gardening, raising berries, working in the orchard and making quilts.

Jake was remembered as a shiftless lout, given to hard drink, harder language and occasional violence. Yet somehow the odd couple raised a fine daughter—Molly. As she grew up, all the boys came to like her. Trouble was, Jake liked her too. When Molly was 16, her father molested her and got her in trouble. The sheriff threw him into the St. Johnsbury jail.

While Jake was incarcerated, Molly's baby—perhaps mercifully—died. To prevent further incidents, Sally sent Molly to a trade school in Massachusetts.

Eventually Jake went free for lack of evidence and by casting doubts on the morality of his wife *and* daughter.

But when he returned home, things had changed. Sally began subjecting him to the worst kind of nagging a person can get—silent hatred. She cooked for him, washed his clothes, raised their fruit and made her quilts, but she never said another word to her husband.

In time, Jake grew unnerved by the relentless silence and dark, hateful looks. His condition worsened when Sally began leaving seemingly innocent and unconnected notes for Jake to find. "Get arsenic for currant bugs," one said. Later, another read, "Best given to him in oatmeal on a cold morning."

So Jake became afraid to eat. He grew nervous. Agitated. Thin as a shadow. One night, a passing neighbor heard angry shouting coming from Jake and Sally's place. Upon approaching, the neighbor found a disheveled Jake, shotgun in hand, obviously drunk and shaking uncontrollably. "She tried to poison me," Jake screamed. "She tried to poison me, so I run her off . . ."

But she didn't run far, because every night after that, Sally would step out of the woods and stare at the house.

Then one day, she vanished altogether. Some thought she'd gone to live with her daughter. Some thought she'd run off with a secret lover. Others thought Jake had killed her.

No matter what became of her, strange things started happening at Jake's place. Something killed his berry bushes. His dog, his only friend, died from poisoning. Someone fired a bullet through his window, missing him by inches.

Now Jake was reduced to a quivering, stuttering skeleton of a man with equal amounts of blood and whiskey in his veins. Every creaking board, every branch scraping a window caused him to jump and shake uncontrollably. A neighbor said he shook so hard it made the whole house tremble.

According to the postmaster, the end came soon afterwards. Someone discovered Jake dead on his own doorstep. He'd been shot through the windpipe. Close by, there was a scrap of paper that said, "Arsenic's too slow."

Everyone in Waterford was convinced Jake's murder was the work of Sally Farr. But no one ever saw her again. At least not until someone noticed the solitary specter of a woman standing, staring at the quivering house.

And people kept seeing her.

She'd appear and vanish mysteriously, while the old house shivered, as if the terrified spirit of its last occupant was trapped forever inside.

HAUNTED SPOTS

JUST AS VERMONT HAS A NUMBER OF NONPOLITICAL DIVISIONS—like unorganized towns and gores—the ethereal Vermont has a number of haunted spots.

Where do we find them? Well, a good place to start might be wherever you find . . .

Ghostly Graves

MY FATHER, who believed in the humor of repetition, would always ask the same question whenever we drove past any Vermont graveyard.

"How many dead in that cemetery?"

I'd start to estimate, then I'd remember. For the hundredth time, I'd answer, "They're all dead."

It was a good joke, I suppose, but I've come to think it might not be exactly true. You see, strange things happen in Vermont cemeteries, usually after dark. And if you're brave enough to venture among the monuments at night, who knows what you might encounter?

One grisly story concerns a remarkable tomb placed in the center of St. Michael's churchyard in Brattleboro. Parishioners erected the vault in memory of their much-beloved organmaster. He had played in their church for nearly half a century.

The story goes that his tomb contained a real organ and that, after death, the organmaster's corpse was entombed, seated at the keyboard.

Shortly after the burial, some of the parishioners were surprised to hear sounds of the organ in the middle of the night. They might have continued to enjoy their organist's posthumous performances, except for one thing: in death he seemed to have lost his ability to play.

Though night after night he apparently kept practicing, his playing got worse and worse. Finally, the only sound was one long mournful note.

We can only guess what the frightened townspeople suspected when they decided to investigate. With flickering candles and blazing torches, they followed the melancholy tone through the darkened churchyard. Cautiously they approached the mausoleum. A couple of the braver among them crept up to the vault. Slowly they pushed open the heavy door and risked a look inside.

A ghastly sight met their eyes. It both explained and deepened the mystery. In the darkness, two rats blinked red eyes at the candle before continuing to feast on the organmaster's fingers.

But surely rats can't explain the more recent and far stranger events that took place in the St. John's Roman Catholic Cemetery in Northfield. It happened in the late 1960s.

A lifelong Northfield resident tells of a Halloween night when he and a bunch of his high school friends had a few beers and headed out to the cemetery in search of some Halloween chills. What he experienced was less like a chill and more like an Arctic wind.

The boys were hiding among the stones hooting and moaning and trying to scare each other.

The man recalls, "It's pitch black and windy and I'm near this huge statue of the Holy Madonna. The other guys are down at the other end hiding. Then I hear these noises, like digging. I turn and see this old guy shoveling away. There was this weird glow around him.

"Then—I swear this—I saw the head of the Madonna turn slowly towards me. That's when I got the hell out!"

What could have caused such a pair of unearthly visions?

"It couldn't have been the beer," the man says. "That stuff doesn't make you hallucinate. Hallucinate wasn't even a word back then."

The disapproving Madonna is relatively new to Vermont ghost lore, but Northfield's Phantom Grave Digger has been on the scene for years. Usually he's spotted with his pick and shovel, standing beside a glowing lantern or walking among the headstones.

Phantom Grave Diggers are one thing, but what about Phantom Grave Robbers?

If they exist, we may have one possible explanation for an especially perplexing mystery that occurred in Greensboro.

The events began in the 1880s, when the body of a man was buried in the Greensboro town cemetery. This interment took place well after Vermont's epidemic of medical grave robbings, so the corpse lay undisturbed for almost one hundred years. Then one night in 1968, somebody opened the grave!

Phantom or physical, the intruder dug down to the coffin, carefully collecting the displaced dirt on a tarpaulin.

When the disturbance was discovered, no one could offer any explanation. Why would someone open a hundred-year-old grave? Who would do such a thing? For what reason? And for heaven's sake, why was it dug up so carefully?

What's even stranger is that the coffin was exposed but it wasn't opened.

To this day, as far as I know, no one can explain this graveyard mystery.

All we can do is ask a thousand questions. Questions like, "How many dead in that cemetery?"

The Devil's Barn

THIS ESPECIALLY GRUESOME EPISODE OF VERMONT HISTORY has all the sinister ingredients of a horror film. It's the story of four evil men whose separate trails of depravation and death crossed the American continent and descended on the tiny Vermont town of Waterford. There each man would encounter a personal hell-on-earth within the walls of an innocent-looking barn.

Events began around 1820 in Baton Rouge, Louisiana. There a privileged young man named Terrance Blunt stole $10,000 from his rich father and vanished. He would squander that money, then steal more whenever he needed it.

Meanwhile a gambler—actually a cheater and swindler—named Andrew Marr buried a fortune near Rochester, New York, then set out on a journey to acquire another ill-won hoard.

Some time later, on the West Coast, a baby-faced serial killer named Calvin Longstreet took the life of a beautiful woman. This was the latest in a series of murders that began with a renowned actress—his own mother.

The fourth player in our odyssey of the fates is Fat Frank Ballard, a rotund, affable bully and successful thief. After beating and robbing an innkeeper in Des Moines, Iowa, Fat Frank made his run.

Over the next fifteen years, leaving a meandering trail of dead bodies and vanished money behind them, the four eventually ended up in the Green Mountain State.

Andrew Marr and Fat Frank Ballard, the gambler and the thief, were the first to meet. Their paths crossed at the St. Johnsbury Fair—then a target for con games and con men.

The two formed an unholy alliance and settled in.

During the year between fairs, they became known as local characters. Frequently visiting general stores in the area, they pretended to be government surveyors, telling colorful tales of high adventure. They probably offered ample—and insightful—commentary on the rising crime rate in the area.

The next summer, in his Albany, New York, hotel room, serial killer Cal Longstreet read about the St. Johnsbury Fair. He imagined the voluptuous forms of beautiful young fairgoers and saw opportunity. Longstreet saddled up and headed for Vermont.

Along the way, somewhere near Rutland, he teamed up with Terrance Blunt. Blunt was whining about hard times and said he was heading for the fair to try the games of chance. Of course there was no way for him to know his luck had all but run out. Fate was pulling these four fiends together; destiny was moving in for the kill.

For the citizens of the St. Johnsbury area, the first week of the fair was memorable—and for all the wrong reasons. A crime wave of robberies and violence had seized the county, leaving no one untouched. Generous rewards were offered for the apprehension of the perpetrator. The amount increased, and "Dead or Alive" was added to the wanted posters after three young women were found raped and murdered. Each had a silk scarf around her neck. Vermonters couldn't know that a scarf was Cal Longstreet's trademark.

But one man knew, for he had witnessed the murder of a kind-hearted local farmgirl named Tessie Bowden. And thus Fate gave another tug on its line, jerking the four closer to their doom.

One night in Waterford, during a fierce summer storm, the four outlaws targeted the ramshackle Connecticut River farm of Uriah Washburn. Uriah was a crazed religious fanatic, a Millerite, who sometimes saw himself as a vengeful god.

The scene was pure gothic horror. With the dark, moonless air wild with rain and lightning, the four pulled up in a covered wagon to ask for shelter in Uriah's barn. Uriah agreed—for a price—and headed off to preach to the winds and shadows.

Uriah's son, Dabby—a misshapen, clubfooted amateur herbalist—seemed somewhat more congenial. He helped the strangers settle in, found blankets to keep them warm; he even offered them some of his homemade root beer.

Reluctantly the thirsty men accepted, but only because there were no hard spirits available in the Washburn household. As they drank, they noticed that the beverage tasted odd.

"What kinda root you use in this root beer?" Terrance Blunt asked.

Within moments he knew. He jerked from his straw bed, clutching his gut and vomiting his life away.

Fat Frank Ballard's overworked heart gave out with the first jolt of searing pain.

Andrew Marr, knotted in agony, screamed himself to death. Only Cal Longstreet lived long enough to ask why.

Without lifting a finger to help, Dabby explained that he'd seen Longstreet murder Tessie Bowden. "She was always kind to me," he said, "and none of you are any good. God'll reward me for what I done . . ."

Then Dabby cut lengths of rope with which he hung the corpses like deer from the central beam of the barn.

When Uriah returned to his barn at first light, he saw the lifeless criminals. Dabby stood nearby, beaming with pride.

Later, father and son went into town to collect the reward money offered for the murderers, leaving their bounty on display as if in warning to others.

And, strangest of all, it was as if a power greater than Dabby's wanted to reinforce that warning. For long after the bodies were removed and buried, and long after the Washburns' ramshackle house had fallen to ruin, people passing the barn at night often saw four dangling corpses silhouetted in the pale light of the full moon.

Terrance Blunt, Andrew Marr, Cal Longstreet, and Frank Ballard did much to secure the honors for vice and skulduggery in the field of masculine effort. Perhaps they have become acquainted by now in some plushy glade in space, call it Hell, Time, Middle Mist, or even Purgatory, where the damned are supposed to writhe.

—James Reynolds
Ghosts in American Houses

General Wayne's Second Home

After Ethan Allen and the Green Mountain Boys seized Fort Ticonderoga, General George Washington assigned Anthony Wayne to take over command. Called "Mad" Anthony by his men, Wayne had a reputation for excessive daring. His hearty laugh thundered across the battlefield as, time after time, he placed himself in danger.

But now he was tired of campaigning and scouting; he needed a rest. The new assignment was made to order. Wayne appreciated this opportunity to catch up with his good friends who were stationed there.

In spite of the wretched conditions at the fort, General Wayne was given comfortable living quarters. As an additional perk, there were many handsome young women around who might share them.

In fact, Mad Anthony Wayne must have been so happy there that his ghost decided to return when he died. Even today, he is said to appear occasionally in the dining room of the commandant's quarters. He'll sit at a table studying maps all night long. At dawn he rises, stretches, belches profoundly . . . then vanishes.

Or sometimes his specter is seen relaxing in front of the fireplace, contentedly puffing a pipe and swigging from a pewter mug. Observers say he looks huge and uniformed, exactly as he appears in his portraits.

But as much as Anthony Wayne liked New York and Ticonderoga, he was equally fond of Vermont. He had good friends in the Green Mountains too. He even enjoyed a brief flirtation with a beautiful young woman from Montpelier, Penelope Haynes, daughter of a wealthy landowner.

Perhaps his spirit couldn't decide in which state to spend eternity. For, odd as it seems, Wayne's ghost is also seen here. He may be the only New York ghost with a second home in Vermont.

The only difference is that *here* his ghost appears with two peculiar companions.

The story begins sometime before his assignment at Ticonderoga. Wayne was leading a scouting party through Vermont toward Canada.

Somewhere around Lake Memphremagog, one of his guides told him about a place where bald eagles were nesting. There were, the guides told him, four or five eaglets in the nest.

Wayne wanted a pair. He knew if the birds were taken early, then carefully trained in the art of falconry, they would make excellent hunting companions. Eagerly, Wayne made an expedition to the spot.

Ever the cautious tactician, Wayne surveyed the high rock ledge where the eagle's nest was built. A fully grown parent circled overhead, as if guarding the nest. The other eagles were off somewhere, probably searching for food. From this distance, he could see just two little heads in the nest. However, the eaglets were a bit older than ideal for his purposes.

But he had come this far; Wayne would not return empty-handed. At his command, a bowman brought down the circling bird with a single arrow.

Before the other eagles could return, Wayne rushed up the rocks to remove the youngsters from their nest. He got more of a fight than he'd expected: One of the eaglets lashed out and clawed Wayne's cheek and nose, scarring him for life. The fighting spirit of the scrappy little bird no doubt appealed to the General.

In the months that followed, Wayne raised the birds himself, handling every facet of their falconry training. His name for them collectively was "North West Passage."

"This one is North," he'd explain in a show of Colonial wit, "and that one is West. Their surname is Passage. I call them that because of the hard time we had finding them."

He kept the birds with him until they died of old age. Over the years, a three-way bond had formed that would survive the grave. For after General Anthony Wayne died in 1796, people started seeing his phantom form in the vicinity of the old log fort and elsewhere around Lake Memphremagog.

Just as in life, Wayne appears extraordinarily large. He's dressed in leather scouting gear as he walks along the shore. Numerous witnesses have seen him alone; others see him with his arms outstretched, one twin bald eagle sitting on each wrist.

And more than one unbelieving observer has seen this strange, ghostly sight become even stranger. Occasionally, when the moon is right and the shadows are long, the spectral General will pause, turn, and face the lake. Then, as if spotting something appealing on the far shore, the General's ghost will decide to cross. He does so at any point simply by walking across the surface of the water.

Strange indeed. But then again, perhaps not so strange. Quite possibly, ghosts just can't swim.

Haunted Hartland

THE TOWN OF HARTLAND on the Connecticut River seems to be a quiet place. Historically, it was once a booming mini-metropolis filled with factories and shops. For a time 150 years ago, it was the second-wealthiest and fourth-largest community in the state. The coming of the railroads put a stop to that. Today, Hartland's main function seems to be keeping Hartford separate from Windsor.

But Hartland deserves to be famous: it seems to have the highest ghost population of any town in the state. Judging by research done by Dick Stillson at the University of Vermont, Hartland has a ghost for every era of the town's history.

In pre-Colonial days, before the Europeans came, the Sumner's Falls area was a popular spot for Abenaki fisherman. The big pool below the falls and the falls itself were perfect for salmon fishing. Evidence of many Indian camps found there suggest it was a special place. And, as is so often the case with ghosts, they hate to leave a place they like.

Over the years, many people fishing the Connecticut have stopped at Sumner's Falls. Sometimes they camp on the shoreline overnight. There, visitors and numerous Hartland residents have witnessed strange sights. In the waters around the falls, they sometimes see dark, moving shapes that appear to be canoes filled with shadowy men. The apparitions never make noise, even as they become momentarily visible, paddling across the reflection of the moon on the water.

Other campers, thinking they're alone at the water's edge, are occasionally surprised to see another campfire a ways off down the shoreline. If they dare approach their neighbors, they might be startled to discover an Indian camp that simply hadn't been there before the sun went down. Generally, these surprised contemporary observers don't stick around to see much of anything else.

Later, after the European takeover, the Connecticut River was used for the great log drives that play such a colorful role in Vermont history. Over the years, many men were lost to the river. Sometimes their bodies were recovered; more often they were never found. Complex currents at the mouths of tributaries were dangerous spots, especially around Sumner's Falls, where at least one logger is known to be buried.

Perhaps some of the old-timers around Hartland still remember all the people who saw—and the few who spoke with—the Ghost Logger of Sumner's Falls. Apparently no one realizes they're speaking to a ghost during the conversation, but a sudden disappearance, a remark from a companion or a recollection of the ghost's anachronistic attire will eventually tip off the witness.

Near the property of Bert Letourneau, a long-time Hartland resident, lies Snail Swamp, described by everyone as an especially eerie place. It feeds into Lulls Brook, which runs beside an old logging road. In the early years of this century, a "plank road" or "log turnpike" was built through the swamp, stretching from Windsor to Woodstock.

For years, a solitary rider, dressed entirely in black, was spotted from time to time, splashing along the rotted timbers of the turnpike, intent on business no living soul could fathom. Those who know the story call him the Phantom Highwayman. The black steed he rides has blazing red eyes and fiery breath.

Who this phantom is—or was—is a mystery, and exactly why he patrols Snail Swamp at night is equally mysterious. People who have seen him say he always travels northwest, heading toward Woodstock. Apparently, he never gets where he is going.

To bring Hartland's ghost lore fully up to date, we have the story of Hartland's Hippie Ghosts. Apparently, the spirits of five young men and two women lurk in the sharp ravine between Garvin and Hartland Hills.

The story is that they were wealthy downcountry students who had rented a house during Christmas break back in 1971. They planned a skiing vacation at Woodstock and Ascutney. According to rumor, they were smoking marijuana and somehow set the house afire. Too stoned to react, all five perished in the blaze.

Local people have reported seeing ghostly longhaired strangers walking on the roadside after dark. A Mr. Sawyer says he saw another phantom with a flaming chair in his arms, running madly from a fire he'll never escape.

Emily's Bridge

MOST STATES CAN BOAST A HAUNTED HOUSE OR TWO. Some even claim to possess the most haunted house in America. But leave it to tiny Vermont to one-up all contenders. Consistent with our picturesque landscape and our contrary nature, we have something no one else can claim—a haunted covered bridge.

Its formal name is the Gold Brook Bridge. Some call it the Stowe Hollow Bridge. But to the people of Stowe, this one-lane, 50-foot structure will always be known as Emily's Bridge. Because Emily is the ghost who haunts it.

Some sources say Emily's is the oldest covered bridge in the country, that its builder, John N. Smith of Moscow, Vermont, designed it with many unique features and bragged it would last forever. Maybe he was right; today, as a historic structure, it is guaranteed perpetual care. What better place for an eternal spirit to take up residence?

Unfortunately, we don't know too much about Emily's life, but there's no shortage of stories about her activities after death. And by most accounts, Emily is none too pleasant.

Night visitors to Emily's Bridge often report weird encounters. While standing on the wooden floor planks, some people hear eerie voices from nowhere uttering words that can never quite be understood. Other times the voice *can* be understood—it sounds like a woman crying for help.

Certain witnesses see flashing white lights. Others experience warm spots in the dead of winter or inexplicable chills in the blistering midsummer heat. Sometimes hats are whisked away when the air is absolutely still. Tourist photographs frequently don't come out, or include puzzling, blurry spots that weren't there when the photo was snapped.

And there are more menacing stories, terrifying dramas played out beneath the dark veils of night. Actions that perhaps reveal Emily's true nature.

For years—until it was stolen—a quaint "Speed Limit" sign said, "Horses at a walk. Motor vehicles, 10 miles per hr."

At such cautious speeds, horses and automobiles were easy prey for Emily's attacks. Sometimes animals crossing the bridge at night were slashed by sharp invisible claws that ripped their hides, leaving long bloody gashes.

When cars replaced horses, the attacks continued. The same claws that wounded horses ruined more than one perfect paint job.

Quite recently, a local man named Vaughn was at Stowe Hollow, sitting in a car with some friends. Peering into the dark cavern of the bridge, he saw a filmy white light shaped like a woman. Everyone was convinced it was Emily. The shape approached the car as the people inside scrambled to lock their doors. For a while the form just hovered there as if staring at the car. It circled the car slowly, gazing into the windows. Then, Vaughn says, it reached out, grabbed the door handle and began shaking the car. One can't be sure if the shaking was attributable to the ghost's strength or tremors of terror experienced by the passengers.

Judging by these episodes, Emily's spirit sounds angry, maybe even insane. But why?

In 1981, a psychic decided to get to the bottom of things. Inside the bridge one night, she lit incense and tried to communicate with Emily's restless ghost. But Emily was in no mood to explain herself; she didn't answer. Apparently, the psychic picked up another set of vibrations. Around 1876, she said, the townspeople had lynched a young *man* on the bridge.

Is there any connection? We'll probably never know (although there *is* a young man in the story, as you'll see).

So far *no one*, psychic, scientist or historian, has been able to prove that Emily actually lived. Or died. But we must remember that in the old days, records—particularly death records—were not always filed. Families routinely buried their dead at home. In certain circumstances, they might not want to talk about a death—especially if it were a suicide.

While *most* stories say that Emily died by her own hand, *all* agree her tragedy occurred on that bridge around 1849.

The best known tale is that Emily was a young Stowe woman who fell for a man who didn't pass muster with her family. Forbidden to marry, the love-struck young couple decided to elope. They planned to meet on the bridge at night. The appointed hour came and went, but the young man never showed up. Shattered, Emily hanged herself from a rafter. And her desperate, angry ghost has haunted the bridge ever since, waiting for her lover to return.

There are variations of the story, but all involve a failed rendezvous and Emily's violent death at the Stowe Hollow Bridge.

I have visited Emily's Bridge several times over the years. Unfortunately, I've never seen anything strange nor have I felt as if I were in the presence of something supernatural.

I must admit I am disappointed. I guess I'm not the young man Emily is waiting for.

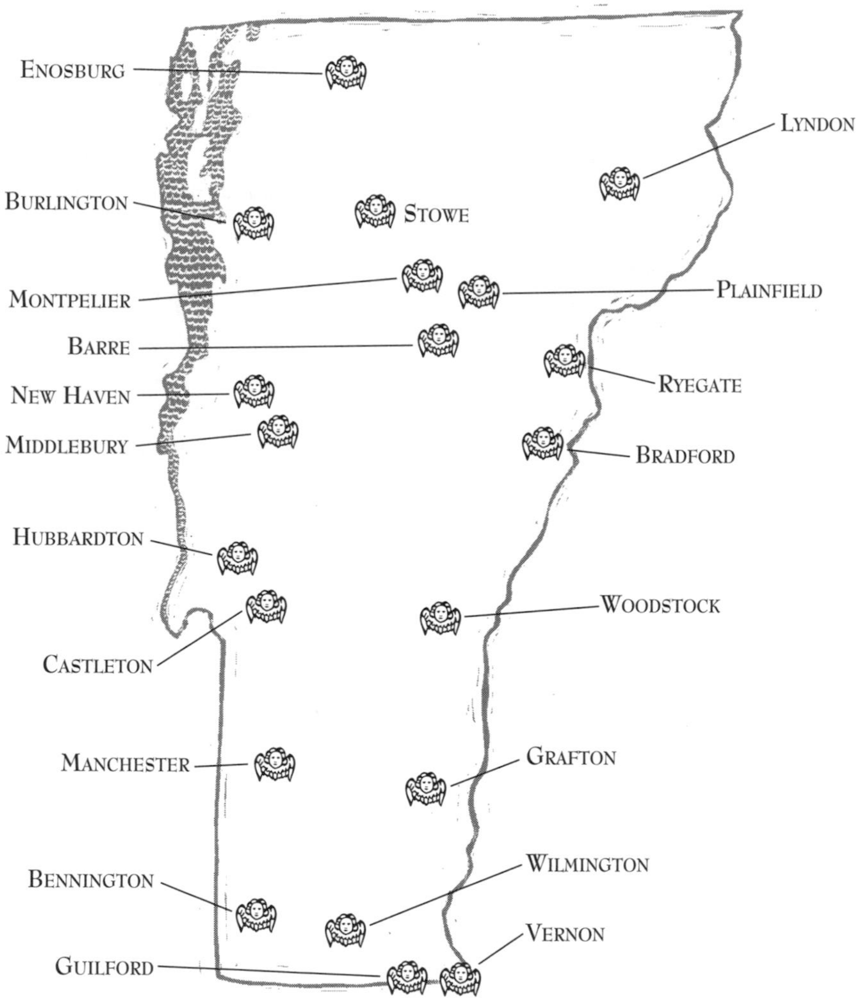

ENOSBURG
LYNDON
BURLINGTON
STOWE
MONTPELIER
PLAINFIELD
BARRE
RYEGATE
NEW HAVEN
MIDDLEBURY
BRADFORD
HUBBARDTON
WOODSTOCK
CASTLETON
MANCHESTER
GRAFTON
WILMINGTON
BENNINGTON
VERNON
GUILFORD

Vampires, Graveyards and Ghouls

DURING 1992, the strangest news story broadcast by WCAX-TV's Channel 3 was about vampirism in Burlington's City Hall Park. Apparently, a gaggle of black-clad youngsters were actually drinking each other's blood right outside Mayor Clavelle's office. The slashing and sipping was reputedly performed under the direction of a 600-year-old master-vampire.

Because the Vermont legislature has never seen the need to create a law that prohibits drinking blood in public, Burlington police couldn't intervene. But when the 600-year-old vampire started flashing a gun, the police took action. Then the boss-vampire did what all vampires do—he vanished.

In this lurid situation, we are, of course, most likely dealing with the delusions of some disturbed teenagers.

But delusion or not, this is nowhere near the first case of vampirism on record in the Green Mountain State.

The Demon Vampire

PERHAPS THE EARLIEST INSTANCE OF VAMPIRISM took place in 1793. It had to do with what locals called "The Demon Vampire." It began in March of 1789 in Manchester, when Captain Isaac Burton married Miss Rachel Harris, a fine, beautiful, and above all healthy, young woman.

Shortly after the wedding, Rachel's health began to fail. The illness was a common one and easily diagnosed: consumption, also called "The White Death." Rachel's health continued to degenerate until February of 1790. Then, less than a year after her wedding, the struggle ended. The lovely young woman died.

In January 1791—less than a year after Rachel's death—Captain Burton married again. This time, his bride was Miss Hulda Powel, another "healthy, good-looking girl" (although many folks held that she was "not as handsome as his first wife").

Soon Hulda, too, began to show the symptoms of consumption: a loss of vitality, an unnatural pallor, fever-flushed cheeks and a persistent, bloody cough. By February 1793, she was in a bad way. Captain Burton and his wife's despairing relatives were ready to try just about anything to save her.

Some well-intentioned Manchester villagers suggested that a vampire had been responsible for Rachel's death and was now having its evil way with Hulda.

Another villager, Timothy Mead, a close friend of the sick woman's father, suggested that it might help to make—as an old account puts it—a "sacrifice to the Demon Vampire." Maybe that would end his feasting on the blood and vitality of the second Mrs. Burton.

And all of a sudden there was hope; maybe they could save the sweet Hulda after all.

In a loathsome ritual—performed more frequently than we might suppose in early New England—Captain Burton's first wife's body was dug up. A year in the grave had left her in a sorry state. Undaunted, Mead and company removed all that remained of her heart, liver and lungs. Then Mead presided over a ceremony in which the unfortunate woman's organs were burned in a blacksmith's forge that, for this one special occasion, was doing double-duty as an altar.

Everyone hoped the morbid ritual would appease the Demon and "effect a cure of the sick second wife."

Predictably, the bizarre ceremony inspired so much interest and curiosity that, according to one source, it was attended by "from five hundred to one thousand people." That's quite a few considering the population of Manchester was only about twelve hundred at that time. But then again, Vermont always has been a tourist state.

Anyway, despite the show of community support and all the efforts made on her behalf, Hulda Burton died less than six months later, on September 6, 1793, a second victim of the Demon Vampire of consumption.

About one hundred years later, the most famous—or at least the most long-lived and publicized—case of Vermont vampirism came to the public's attention. It was reported in the *Boston Transcript* during the first week of October 1890. A more complete accounting of the remarkable events appeared as a page-one story in Woodstock's own newspaper, the *Vermont Standard*. Imagine seeing this headline while sipping your morning coffee: "Vampirism in Woodstock."

The article recalled events that supposedly occurred in the 1830s when a local man named Corwin had died of consumption.

His body was buried in the Cushing Cemetery. A while later, his brother—presumably also named Corwin—began wasting away. Of course the living Corwin may have been showing symptoms of his dead brother's disease. Or, as was the common wisdom, there might have been a more grisly alternative. Perhaps the dead Corwin had come back as a vampire, his spirit rising from the grave every night to feed on the blood of his living brother.

To find out for sure, the town fathers ordered the body disinterred. A horrifying discovery convinced them they were dealing with the supernatural. Dr. Joseph Gallup, the town's leading physician and head of Vermont Medical College, observed that "the vampire's heart contained its victim's blood" (though how he was able to determine that remains a mystery).

There was only one way to stop the spread of evil: concerned parties would assemble on Woodstock's boat-shaped green and perform an exorcism.

Predictably, most of the town's population turned out for the event. Dr. Gallup and Woodstock's other physicians built a fire in the middle of the green, heated up an iron pot and cooked the undecayed heart until it was reduced to ashes.

Then they buried the pot and ashes in a hole 15 feet deep, covered it with a 7-ton slab of granite and, before refilling the hole, sprinkled everything with bull's blood for purification.

Finally, they forced the dying Corwin to swallow a ghastly medicine made of bull's blood mixed with some of his brother's ashes. They believed this concoction would break the vampire's curse and stop the victim's body from wasting away.

Unfortunately, we never learn if Brother Corwin survived the disease, let alone the cure, but the town fathers were convinced they had rid Woodstock of vampirism forever.

As far as I can tell, they were right.

Today we can't help but wonder whether the whole newspaper article was some wild contrivance anticipating Bram Stoker's *Dracula*. Or could there be a drop of truth to some of this bloody business?

Researchers have found that Dr. Gallup, all his colleagues and most of the townspeople mentioned in the newspaper article were real.

On the other hand, Woodstock's records—birth, death, church and property—show no indication of a man called Corwin. And there is no Corwin marker in the Cushing Cemetery.

Nor has anyone been able to locate the 7-ton granite slab, much less the iron pot of ashes supposedly buried somewhere under Woodstock's scenic green.

The White Death

THESE STORIES OF OUR NATIVE VAMPIRES are good examples of how early Vermonters resorted to folk beliefs about ghosts, witchcraft and satanism to come to grips with unexplained events like mysterious illnesses and deaths.

It's not hard to imagine why consumption—or tuberculosis as we call it now—came to be associated with vampirism. TB was the plague of the nineteenth century. In New England alone, the death tolls were staggering. Transmission was facilitated by everyday living conditions: large families, often poorly nourished, who shared crowded quarters for long periods. It was quite normal for the disease to run through families. Highly contagious and invariably fatal, TB was so lethal one physician called it the first disease "to deter practitioners from attempting a cure."

Its vernacular names—consumption and The White Death—tell much about how it affected the victim.

As The White Death progressed, there was indeed a "transformation": the infected person's skin became alabaster pale, ghostly, and translucently thin. A network of light blue veins became visible beneath its surface. There was often a feverish reddening of the cheeks, fainting spells, anemia, weight loss and an increasingly fragile demeanor. Oddly, due to certain romantic notions of the time, these symptoms made the victims, especially young women, strangely alluring while their health and strength were consumed by the disease.

It was probably easy for early Vermonters to imagine this wasting away as the result of a vampire's parasitic kiss, and the mysteriously heightened feminine beauty as evidence of the infernal transformation from victim to vampire.

A seemingly incongruous component of the disease contributed to its mystery: consumptives occasionally experienced surprising bursts of energy. Many were known to have powerful sex drives. These attributes suggested the individuals were clinging to life in a manner that could survive the grave. Dr. Paul Sledzik of the National Museum of Health and Medicine in Washington, D.C., researched the folk reasoning that led to methods of destroying vampirism. "When someone died of consumption, it was believed they could come back from the dead and drain the life force of their living relatives. In order to stop this, family members would go into the grave and somehow attempt to kill the person again."

When relatives opened the coffins of recently dead consumptives, the corpses, formerly thin and frail, were often found to be bloated with pale flesh. Fingernails seemed to have grown into claws, and, perhaps the most damning evidence, blood was often found in the mouth. There are even accounts, Dr. Sledzik says, of bodies jerking and gurgling as the remains were mutilated.

The stake through the heart approach to dispatching vampires was a European tradition, not practiced by New Englanders. Here, the technique was to remove any remaining flesh and burn it. Decapitation was also a popular deterrent. Or simply causing some disruption to the body was thought to be enough to kill a vampire.

Sledzik located several old New England graves from which the bodies had been disinterred, then mutilated. Occasionally, he found skeletons arranged in the familiar symbol of death: long upper leg bones placed in "X" formation on the chest, then topped with the skull—the so-called skull and crossbones.

Today, while walking through Vermont graveyards, it's hard to keep from wondering how many similar rituals went unrecorded. And how many heartless corpses rest beneath our feet.

The Hubbardton Horror

But vampire hunters were not the only ones who disturbed the sleep of deceased Vermonters, as we shall see in this next delightfully grisly graveyard tale. In fact, several decades of ghoulish activity finally culminated on November 29, 1830 with what has come to be known as The Hubbardton Raid.

Picture this: A mob of three hundred angry villagers armed with guns and ax handles marches the five miles from Hubbardton to Castleton. Their frenzy heightens as driving snow blurs their vision and slows their progress. Shouting their demands, the mob storms a two-story clapboard building. A medical building.

Through the window, the marchers can see figures inside, scurrying from room to room, illuminated by fireplaces and kerosene lamps. They're talking frantically among themselves.

Mob leaders step forward, demanding entry, but a doctor puts them off. Finally, the front door is unlocked; farmers and woodsmen rush inside. But they're struck dumb by what they see: human remains scattered everywhere—arms, legs, pieces of flesh. Nearby, they see dissection tools: knives, saws and forceps.

At length, desperate to end the siege before violence erupts, the doctor surrenders two parcels to the crowd—one large, the other small.

The parcels contain parts of a human being.

Sound like the climax of some classic horror movie?

Well, there's more: The crowd had begun its march on the Castleton Medical Academy after an alert sexton discovered something sinister in the Hubbardton cemetery. The flowers he had carefully placed on Mrs. Penfield Churchill's grave had been slightly rearranged. Also, a tiny mark he had made at the grave site had been obliterated.

The sexton knew exactly what these signs meant: the ghouls had struck again. Mrs. Penfield Churchill's grave had been emptied—the work of grave robbers. For the people of Hubbardton, this was the last straw. They'd had enough of these unholy "Resurrectionists" and the heartless doctors they supplied. The Vermonters took action. The Hubbardton Raid began.

Body-snatching?

Grave-robbing?

In idyllic Vermont?

Did such a thing really happen here?

Indeed it did; body-snatching was a big problem all over New England. But for the practitioners—often the medical students themselves—it was a profitable undertaking.

At the time of The Hubbardton Raid, Vermont had *three* medical schools: in Castleton, Woodstock and Burlington. From 1820 to

1840, they taught more than 1,600 students. And fresh bodies were needed to practice on. The ideal ratio was one body per six students, so demand for suitable corpses was high. And the supply was limited—limited to every Vermont graveyard within 20 miles of each school.

To abolish grave-robbing, Vermont tried passing laws that threatened fines, imprisonment, even public flogging. But enforcement was impossible. During the two decades in question, just seven grave robbers were arrested. Only one was convicted. Since the law could do nothing, protecting graves became the family's responsibility. Three safeguards were common: the first, piling stones, logs and tangled twigs above the coffin to make digging slow and difficult; second, locking the bodies in secure vaults close to the cemeteries until putrefaction made them unsaleable. The third option was available only to the wealthy: a family could hire a grave watcher to work from dusk till dawn. After about ten nights, decomposition would end his vigil.

Despite these deterrents, grave-robbing was a relatively safe occupation. Practitioners always worked the night shift. The hours were short; each theft took only about sixty minutes. And cemeteries were usually far enough from town so observation was unlikely. What's more, these midnight intruders were highly skilled; generally they could cover all evidence that a grave had been tampered with.

Here's how they operated. First, they'd contact a medical school to guarantee their market. Then, they'd check out several cemeteries, looking for fresh graves and assessing security precautions. Next, a team of three would arrive by wagon at night. Hauling two tarpaulins, specialized tools and a well-shaded lantern, they'd locate their target. They'd dig a small hole—just 3 feet square. Piling the dirt on an open tarp allowed them to refill the hole quickly without leaving telltale residue.

After exposing the head of the coffin, they used a drill to bore holes in the wood, forming a square that could easily be popped out. A saw might have worked faster, but it would be impossible to use in the confines of such a cramped hole. Of course an ax would be too noisy.

Now, with access to the corpse, these corrupt craftsmen used a specialized tool called "the hook"—a 5-foot pole with handles on one end and a meat hook on the other. They embedded the hook under the corpse's chin, yanked the body out of the coffin and pulled it up through the dirt. Then they used the second tarpaulin to wrap their prize.

An alternate method involved a system of straps. Though slower, straps saved wear and tear on the cadaver.

Which method of extraction was used on Mrs. Penfield Churchill?

Probably the hook. As you recall, when the doctor returned her corpse to the Hubbardton Raiders, he handed it over in two parcels.

I leave you to speculate about which package contained what.

Today, for the most part, grave-robbing is an obsolete skill. But it represents an unsavory part of our past that most Vermonters would like to keep . . . buried.

Grave Concerns

BEFORE WE ESCAPE GRAVEYARDS ALTOGETHER, let's pause and look around a little to see how the monuments and epitaphs give us unique insight into the history of our state and the philosophy of our forefathers.

In the beginning, I suppose tombstones were simply rocks placed over graves to keep the predators away. Then it occurred to somebody that names could be carved into those stones, thus furnishing the interred with their last address.

And finally, in a moment of inspiration, someone discovered that gravestones would be a perfect place to display a final eulogy or to immortalize one's last words.

For example, Ebenezer Scott of Vernon died a grandfather in 1826 at age 83. His survivors used the headstone to summarize his life: "The first white male born in Bernardston, Massachusetts. / Was taken with his mother and two brothers / by the Indians, carried to Quebec, sold to the French / when he was 8 years old. Returned to his father. Served in the Revolution—drew a pension."

Some gravestones merely relate the circumstances of the death.

Thirteen-year-old Abial Perkins of Plainfield drowned in 1826.

The event is remembered this way: "This Blooming Youth in Health Most Fair / To his Uncle's Mill-pond did repaire / Undressed himself and so plunged in / But never did come out again."

Conversely, some people chose to remain anonymous in death. My favorite example comes from Stowe. A stone with no name and no date that simply says: "I was somebody. / Who, is no business / of yours."

Eunice Page of Plainfield died in 1888. The granite accounting of her life is not without an element of mystery. "Five times five years I lived a virgin's life, / Nine times five years I lived a virtuous wife, / Wearied of this mortal life, I rest." She died at age 73. Makes you wonder what she was up to during the three years unaccounted for.

Certain stones told the world how much a loved one would be missed. Check out this one from West Cemetery in Middlebury. It's on the stone of Edward Oakes who died in 1866, aged 24. It says, "Faithful husband thou art / At rest untill we meet again." Sounds like Mrs. Oakes has plans for Edward . . .

Stones were also used to articulate religious and philosophical positions. This irreverent view was expressed by George F. Spencer on his own monument in Lyndon Center: "Beyond the universe there is nothing and within the / universe the supernatural does not and cannot exist. / Of all deceivers who have plagued mankind, none are so / deeply ruinous to human happiness as those impostors who / pretend to lead by a light above nature. / Science has never killed or persecuted a single / person for doubting or denying its teachings, and / most of these teachings have been true; but religion / has murdered millions for doubting or denying her / dogmas, and most of these dogmas have been false."

More befitting Vermont taciturnity is the gravestone of Charles Bowker who died in 1874 and rests in Restland Cemetery, Wilmington. His stone simply says, "It is all right."

Obviously, the old timers had a different way of relating to death than we do today. For them, death was more immediate, a constant companion.

When loved ones passed on, their bodies were kept at home, prepped by the family and laid out in the parlor, until buried. Later, the funeral business relieved the family of dealing with the deceased. Professional undertakers prepped the body, then laid it out in a parlor of their own, giving birth to the term "funeral parlor."

And so began the process of distancing ourselves from death, sanitizing it, and trying to forget about it until we are forced to take notice.

Our changing attitudes about mortality are nowhere better expressed than on gravestones. Our ancestors' monuments kept the memory of the deceased alive, but solemn mottoes carved there often reminded the living "Your days, too, are numbered."

Take the tragedy expressed on twin stones in Grafton. The first says: "In Memory of Thomas K. Park Jr. and thirteen infants: Youth behold and shed a tear / Se[e] fourteen children slumber here. / Se[e] their image how they shine / Like flowers of a fruitful vine." Beside it is the stone of Thomas Park's wife, Rebecca, who died in 1803 at age 40. "Behold and se[e] as you pass by. / My fourteen children with me lie. / Old or young you soon must die. / And turn to dust as well as I."

A grim fatalism. But often the same fatal reminder was expressed with a sort of defiant "graveyard humor."

This epitaph was reported around 1880 in Barre above the grave of Solomon Pease. It read: "Under the sod and under the trees / Lies the body of Solomon Pease / He is not here, there's only pod; / Pease shelled out and went to God."

I think we can be pretty sure the humor was intentional. I'm less certain about this instance, reportedly from a Burlington, Vermont, cemetery: "Here lies our darling baby boy, / He never cries nor hollers. / He lived for one and twenty days / And cost us forty dollars."

Death is certain, but the afterlife is another thing entirely.

Postmortem uncertainty was succinctly stated on the stone of Mary S. Hoyt of Bradford who died in 1836: "She lived—what more can then be said: / She died—and all we know she's dead."

Equally uncertain was Alden Work, a merchant and legislator from Ryegate who died at 80. "I lived on Earth / I died on Earth / In Earth I am interred. / All that have life / Are sure of Death / The rest may be inferred."

And yet a *kind* of certainty is expressed in the last words on the stone of Henry Clay Barney of Guilford who died in 1915 at age 82.

He says: "My life's been hard / And all things show it; / I always thought so / And now I know it."

This last epitaph is impossible to categorize. A man from Enosburg Falls named Church outlived four wives. He decided to move their remains closer to his home. But during the digging, the bones of the four women got hopelessly mixed together. So Mr. Church had a new headstone carved that said: "Stranger pause and drop a tear / For Emily Church lies buried here / Mixed in some perplexing manner / With Mary, Martha and probably Hannah."

If we turn our attention from epitaphs to the monuments themselves, we make some remarkable discoveries.

For example, Vermont's only royalty is buried in Middlebury's West Cemetery. Walking past the grave of Charlotte Moody, and before reaching Caroline Mead's, there is a headstone bearing a surprising date. It says the grave's occupant died in 1883—*B.C.*! 1883 B.C.? Is that a slip of the stonecutter's chisel?

A closer look reveals it's the grave of Amun-Her-Khepesh-Ef, the 2-year-old son of an ancient Egyptian king. But why is he buried in Middlebury, Vermont?

More than a century ago, Henry Sheldon, an oddities collector from Middlebury, bought the child's mummy from a New York dealer. After Sheldon's death, the museum that now bears his name stored the mummy until 1945 when the curator rediscovered it. George Mead, president of the museum's board of directors, decided to give the little prince a proper Christian burial. He had the mummy cremated and buried the ashes in his own family plot—sort of a postmortem adoption, I suppose.

In nearby New Haven, the grave of Timothy Clark Smith has long been a local curiosity. Smith was born in Monkton and later traveled around the world in the foreign service. But he was back in Vermont, staying at the Middlebury Inn, when he died.

Because of grisly things he'd heard and seen in his travels, Smith had developed a terrible fear of being buried alive. His family knew this, so they left him where he was and continued paying rent on his room at the inn. Eventually, the authorities stepped in and demanded that

Smith be buried. His corpse was moved to a vault at New Haven's Evergreen Cemetery where round-the-clock guards stood watch in case Smith should come back to life.

Meanwhile, a very special grave was being prepared for him.

When Smith was finally laid to rest, his face was positioned beneath a cement tube that led to the surface. The tube was covered with a 14-by-14-inch square of plate glass, his window to the world. And in the corpse's hand, they placed a bell that he could ring if he chanced to wake up and find he'd been buried alive. As far as I know, that bell has never sounded.

Down south in Bennington, we have the strange case of a Mrs. Bartlett, who gained a lot of weight—after she died! During 1870, a group of workmen were relocating bodies in a local cemetery. When they got to Mrs. Bartlett's grave, they ran into trouble. The corpse just wouldn't budge. The poor woman had been in the ground only about twelve years, but in that time, for some unknown reason, her corpse had turned to stone. The petrified body now weighs more than 500 pounds. You might say that Mrs. Bartlett is her own gravestone.

Perhaps the most frightening graveyard tale comes from Montpelier. It has to do with an especially elegant monument erected around 1930. It's a dark bronze statue of the Virgin Mary, seated, with her sorrow-filled face upturned toward Heaven. Somewhere along, she picked up the nickname "Black Agnes."

While the origins of the "Black Agnes" legend are vague, one lingering rumor is that she guards the grave of a murder victim. Apparently, there's a curse connected to the gravestone, for it is said that anyone who sits on Black Agnes's lap in the light of the full moon will suffer seven years of bad luck, and maybe even death.

As you might expect, there are a few stories—all lacking specifics—illustrating that the curse really works. One is about a certain high school boy who defied the curse by sitting on Agnes's lap. Shortly afterward—and well within the fatal seven years—he died in a canoeing accident on the Winooski River less than half a mile from Agnes.

I asked a few people around Montpelier if they've ever sat on Black Agnes's lap. I couldn't find anyone who had, but plenty of people assured me they had not!

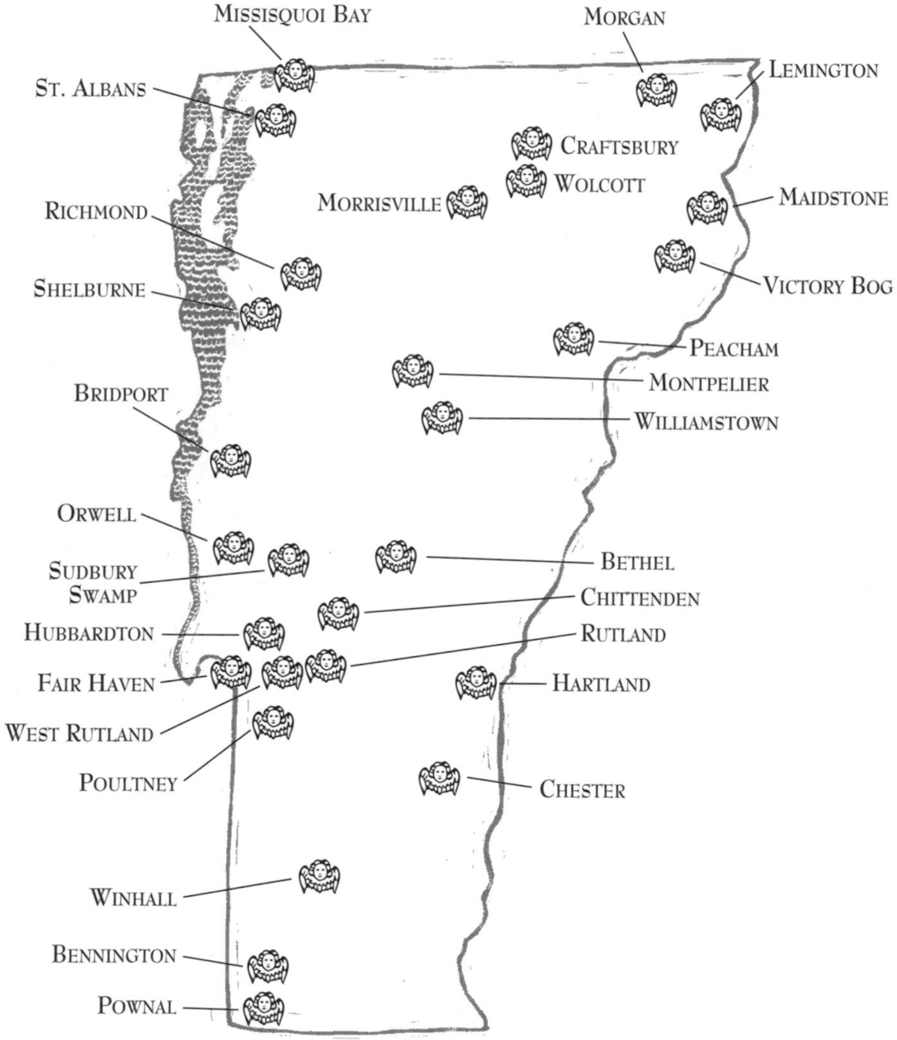

Missisquoi Bay
Morgan
St. Albans
Lemington
Craftsbury
Wolcott
Morrisville
Maidstone
Richmond
Victory Bog
Shelburne
Peacham
Montpelier
Bridport
Williamstown
Orwell
Bethel
Sudbury Swamp
Chittenden
Hubbardton
Rutland
Fair Haven
Hartland
West Rutland
Poultney
Chester
Winhall
Bennington
Pownal

Whose Woods Are These?

Vermonters are always seeing weird things in the woods: leprechauns near Montpelier, black panthers and tawny-colored catamounts just about everywhere, the terrifying Bennington Monster, the mysterious Goonyak. And, of course, Champ, that benign and beneficent denizen of Lake Champlain—who, believe it or not, has been sighted on land several times.

Considering the number of Green Mountain monsters, Vermont should be one of the scariest places in the world.

Oddly though, when we go looking for monsters, they're not around.

That's the frustrating thing about monster-hunting: either there's no monster to be found, or you catch a fleeting glimpse of some unusual critter, then it slips away and is gone forever.

Big Birds and Bad Beasts

A fleeting glimpse . . . Case in point: the town of Hartland has a tradition of monster sightings dating back to the eighteenth century. The "hot spot" is the area of Skunk Hollow Valley and Densmore Hill. Known locally as the "Densmore Hill Monster," the mystery beast has a strange manner of locomotion; it doesn't walk or fly, it *slithers*. Although this vaguely described creature isn't spotted much anymore, there may be a few old-timers who claim to have seen it. The stories start when Thomas Rood settled on Densmore Hill in 1763. Local legend holds that Rood's son had a run-in with the monster. It carted off his wife and apparently prompted his suicide. Rood never had an opportunity to describe the beast, but others have said that it's huge and in some ways resembles a bear. Not a very helpful description.

And gone forever . . .

Recently I talked with a woman who once lived in Shelburne. She told me about the day she looked out her kitchen window and saw a huge bird in her backyard. Its head was a good 3 to 4 feet off the ground, its neck was long and thin and its aspect was somehow . . . unpleasant, maybe even sinister. She had never seen anything like it. The only birds she could compare it to were the vultures she used to see in cowboy movies—but this was bigger. And decidedly stranger.

It was especially unsettling, she said, because as she looked at it, it was looking back at her, staring, never breaking eye contact.

Things got "curiouser and curiouser" when it flew off. She figured a bird that size would need a running start. But no. This creature just rose into the air and soared off among the trees. Its flight was especially perplexing because its wingspan was from 8 to 10 feet, greater than the distance between many of the tree trunks. Yet the bird flew without colliding with any of them. The witness told me she phoned experts at various schools and colleges, but no one had any idea what she might have seen.

Unfortunately, there were no other reported sightings, so, understandably, she stopped telling people about it. She swears she saw something, but has no idea what.

The Bennington Monster

ANOTHER RARE BIRD, so to speak, may still be glimpsed occasionally in the southwestern part of the state. Glastenbury Mountain, near Bennington, has long been considered one of Vermont's most haunted spots. Some people remember the area as the scene of eight of the state's most mysterious disappearances during the late '40s and early '50s (see "The Mystery of the Bennington Triangle"). But long before that, many of the earliest settlers reported strange lights, indistinct forms, frightening sounds and unaccountable, unidentifiable odors. To this day, some of the people living in the hills swear their forefathers were not imagining things when they claimed to have encountered monstrous animals—prehistoric or maybe preternatural—along the thickly wooded paths or deep within the undeveloped forest.

One especially frightening tale comes from the nineteenth century, when a stagecoach line passed along the ridges of Woodford and Glastenbury mountains. Although the participants' names are long forgotten, their story is etched in the folk memory of the region.

On one unforgettable nighttime run, the stage driver was forced to slow down when a sudden, heavy rainfall ripped open the sky. The deluge was so fierce it washed out large sections of the road, eventually forcing the driver to a complete stop amid the dark wilderness.

The horses bucked and whinnied, almost in a panic. The driver, fearing a bobcat, grabbed his rifle and climbed down. There, in the pale light of his lantern, he saw huge circular imprints in the damp ground.

Exploring with his lantern, he saw how the imprints formed a line of tracks, as if something gigantic had passed by. And, he reasoned, just moments ago, or the rain would have washed the imprints away.

His heart quickened as he examined the tracks. Not only were they fresh, they were widely spaced and deep! The frightened driver

concluded that if they were made by an animal, it must be tremendous in size—very different from anything he had ever encountered.

He called to the passengers. He wanted them to see the tracks and help him determine what manner of animal might be in their midst.

Just then the horses reared and screamed.

A savage, thunderous blow toppled the wooden carriage.

Four terrified passengers huddled with the driver, quaking in fear.

As cold rain pelted them, they stared up at two large glowing eyes watching them from the nearby wood. A huge beast, partly obscured by tree branches and darkness, roared again and tramped off into the night, leaving the travelers silent and stricken with horror.

This beast, whatever it may be, has become known as the Bennington Monster. We can only speculate about where it came from or where it went, but it is easy to see how the topography of the area might give birth to legends, if not actual monsters. Historically, the bogs and ponds of Beaver Meadows on Woodford Mountain were considered a likely lair for the monsters. Another suspected haunt was Pine Valley, whose swamps and thickets stretch from Woodford to Manchester.

Today, the mountains are every bit as wild and mysterious. They're inaccessible, full of dark places, jutting outcroppings and vast marshlands bordered by silent ponds or deep, quiet channels.

Monster advocates may still believe the creatures sprawl in these swamps, feeding and soaking up the sun before beginning their frightful midnight treks through the unpopulated forest.

An interesting footnote to the story occurred in 1934 when proof of the Bennington Monster was finally discovered—or so people thought.

Workers at "Bar" Harbor's sandpit on the lower slope of Bald Mountain unearthed a number of large bones that they assumed had come from a much larger skeleton.

News of the find spread rapidly through all the towns in the area. By the time the story got to Old Bennington, the bones were reported to have come from a "Brontosaurus Rex."

Alas, when the fossils were examined by more knowledgeable eyes, they were identified as having come from a cow.

But a BIG one.

Goonyak— The Monster from Nowhere

There are a few stories in which the monster doesn't escape or remain as mysterious as the Bennington Beast. One such tale was told around Montpelier in 1978. It involved some sort of entity—savage, gigantic and impossibly alien—that was shot to death by a Fish and Game Department Warden from Craftsbury. The creature's corpse was hauled off to a secret laboratory on the fourth floor of a building at the University of Vermont in Burlington. There, experts performed an autopsy while armed guards kept curiosity seekers away.

This tantalizing tale most likely originated in the sparsely populated Morrisville-Wolcott-Craftsbury area. There certain people claimed to know about the monster; they even had a name for it—Goonyak.

The sequence of events that brought Goonyak to public attention is a little hard to reconstruct. But as word about the monster spread, terror and uncertainty blossomed. Mounting tension eventually culminated in a public meeting where people gathered to give testimony.

There bits of the truth came to light. For example, one of the first to hear about Goonyak was a 21-year-old man named John Maskell, a new employee at the Pratt and Read Corporation in Morrisville. Maskell was enjoying a drink of water when another employee, an older man named Morris Shulham, approached him.

There is no record of what was said, but based on Maskell's testimony, their conversation went something like this:

"Hey, d'you hear that weird stuff on the radio this morning?" Shulham asked.

"No. What stuff?"

"About some monster. Goonyak, they called it."

Maskell grew interested. "No. I didn't hear anything about a monster. What kind of monster?"

"Didn't hear it, eh? Been on the radio the last couple mornings. Fella says some kind of queer cussed critter busted into a barn somewheres around Craftsbury. North Wolcott, maybe it was. Happened about four in the morning. Farmer—I forget his name—was on his way out to do his chores . . ."

Shulham continued, telling how the farmer had discovered his barn door ripped off its hinges. Then he found a broken partition behind which he kept his prize Holstein bull.

When the farmer heard an odd cry from outside, he figured the bull had crashed out of his stall, slammed through the barn door and was running amok in the farmyard.

The farmer heard the unfamiliar cry again—he said it sounded like an elephant, only louder—and ran to get his rifle. As he raced to the far side of the barn, he encountered a sight that froze the blood in his veins.

There, crossing the farmyard, was a monstrous humanoid 8 feet tall. It was dragging the lifeless body of the 1000-pound bull. The farmer could see the bull's neck had been broken. Apparently, Goonyak had yanked the bull out of its stall, snapped its neck, then started dragging it across the field. As Goonyak trudged onward, the farmer watched it ripping off part of the bull's face with its 6-inch claws.

Angry, unbelieving, the farmer started shooting. Impossible as it sounds, Goonyak took ten shots in the chest with a 30.06 rifle before it died.

As this dramatic story spread, variations began to appear. Among them, how a game warden shot Goonyak, and how the monster's body was secretly autopsied at UVM. Somehow, the name of a real warden became associated with the case: John Kapusta of Craftsbury.

Shortly, the episode came to the attention of the Vermont Fish and Game Department (as the Fish and Wildlife Department was called until 1983). A supervisor, John Hall, contacted Kapusta to learn if it were true.

It's completely false, Kapusta assured him. And with that, the legend of Goonyak began to fall apart.

A check with Chief Medical Examiner Dr. Eleanor McQuillen and professors of animal pathology and zoology at UVM resulted in amused but negative responses—there had been no autopsy.

A check with several of the area's radio stations revealed there had been no broadcast. And of course there was no irate farmer or dead bull.

When at last a public fact-finding meeting was conducted in Craftsbury, many discrepancies were evident in various versions of the story. Descriptions of what Goonyak looked like, its actions, and how it died varied with the teller. But one fact was universal: no one had any hard evidence.

The consensus was that Goonyak did not exist.

So where did such a story come from?

Game wardens speculated that someone had seen the skinned carcass of a bear. Something like that could appear half-human at a glance. In any event, they guessed, the myth was probably conjured up by a deer hunter.

And our storyteller Morris Shulham was a deer hunter. Whether Shulham's the culprit or someone else, the creator of Goonyak is like his creation—part of a vanishing breed. I'm talking about good old Yankee yarn-spinners, practitioners of an art form I hope will never become obsolete.

That Darned Cat

NOT EVERY VERMONT MONSTER is a hoax or figment of the storyteller's imagination. Take another strange critter that continues to haunt the Green Mountain wilderness. Not as alien as Goonyak or the Bennington Monster, this elusive animal has long provided one of the state's most lively and enduring controversies.

I'm talking about Vermont's own version of the Cheshire cat, an oversized feline that repeatedly appears and vanishes, leaving witnesses scratching their heads and wondering what they have seen. This mystery cat has several names: mountain lion, cougar, panther and, perhaps most colorful, catamount.

Most so-called experts will tell you the catamount became extinct in Vermont when Alexander Crowell shot the last one in Barnard back in 1881. Crowell's cat, known as the "Barnard Monster," is still here; it's on display at the Vermont Historical Society Museum in Montpelier—stuffed.

But do live cats still roam the Vermont hills?

In the absence of proof (a live specimen, a carcass, the plaster cast of a track, or an indisputable photograph, the Fish and Wildlife Department continues to maintain there are no resident catamounts in Vermont.

Yet people keep spotting them!

• In the early 1980s, a state forestry employee and level-headed woodsman caught the cat in his headlights while driving through Victory Bog in the wilds of the Northeast Kingdom.

• Mary Charland of Bridport saw the panther several times between 1986 and 1991. Once she saw it rolling in the dirt road by her house. This dirt bath presumably was to drive off fleas. "He's a beautiful cat," she said. "He's big and has a long tail and long legs and a beautiful head."

• Bridport Farmer Charles Deering saw the cat around 1989. He recalled it as about 4 feet long with a 5-foot stride. He said it was like a mountain lion in color and appearance.

• In 1990, a high school teacher from St. Albans saw one from the porch of his home on Bushey Road. It crossed the lawn beside his house, leaped over a fence and sailed halfway across the road before vanishing into a corn field. The teacher admits he had no idea what he had seen until later when he chanced to hear a radio program about New England panther sightings.

• In 1991, a Burlington writer and his wife saw a catamount crossing Interstate 89 near Bethel. The cat stopped at the side of the road and glanced casually at their oncoming car before springing into the bushes.

• Orwell resident Sharon Pinsonneault saw it on August 21, 1991, crossing Route 22A near the Benson-Orwell line. "I had no idea what it was," she said. "The thing I remember is the tail. It almost reached the ground and it curled up in an arch."

• Dorothy Catchapaw of Duxbury recalls an incident in 1924 or 1925 when she was 12 years old and living on her grandfather's farm in Fays Corner, near Richmond. Her 10-year-old brother had been tending the cows in the pasture. He ran into the house terribly frightened. Catchapaw tells what her brother saw: "He said it was a big cat with a long tail. He said it was up in a tree [near] where the cows were. The color was darker than a yellow cat. My father and I went back with him to the pasture. He showed us the tree the cat was in, and there were the claw marks of a big cat on the tree. That night, the cry of the cougar was heard by many."

• Marian Harpan Peduzzi of Montpelier recently reported having seen the more elusive *black panther* in 1946 when she was 16 years old. Her suspenseful encounter began as she was walking on Vine Street, a dirt road near U.S. 302 in Berlin. It was about four o'clock, and she was heading home for supper:

"As I looked to my right . . . my gaze fell upon what looked to be a black labrador," she said. "Then I saw it scratching backwards with its hind legs at the ground. Strange behavior for a dog. . . . Next, I observed that the head and jaws seemed to be very large—larger than those of a retriever."

Walking with great caution now, she hoped to reach her friend Mrs. Tiffin's house.

"The animal was perhaps 100 to 150 yards out in that field, and the wind was blowing my way. My heart was pounding, but I was not panicking. . . . If that cat could smell me and wanted a meal, then I'd be trapped."

She climbed the porch steps and knocked on the door. *What if nobody's home*? she thought as she called, "Mrs. Tiffin, Mrs. Tiffin."

Finally, Mrs. Tiffin came to the door. "I quickly told her I thought there was a panther out there. . . . She looked. She agreed. It looked more like a cat than a dog . . . a very big black cat.

"As we stood there, the panther stood up . . . and loped directly toward the house. . . . Then . . . leaving about 30 feet of lawn between us, it veered to the right and cantered parallel to the road, and we saw it full view, a Vermont black panther, a catamount, in all its glory. . . . He was about 4 feet long, plus carrying a long tail which curved to the ground and up as he traveled. . . . Truly an elegant animal, sleek and glossy in the sun, he was."

And the sightings go on and on.

As far as I know, the first person to start systematically collecting panther stories was Reverend William Ballou of my hometown, Chester. He had discovered panther tracks in the snow while leading a group of Boy Scouts over Stedman Hill. The tracks were 5 inches across. Judging from the snow's broken crust, Rev. Ballou estimated the animal weighed at least 175 pounds.

Subsequently, he founded his "Panther Club" which met for the first time on May 18, 1934, at the Fullerton Inn (now the Inn At Long Last). Membership was limited to those who had seen a panther or its tracks or had heard one yell. The meetings were always well attended.

In the following years, people from all over the state have kept reporting giant cats from 4 to 7 feet long. The reports are so convincing that enlightened lawmakers have placed catamounts on Vermont's endangered species list.

Stranger still, we seem to have two varieties of "big cat" roaming the state: the tawny-colored catamount and the more evasive black panther. We have no way of knowing if we're dealing with two distinct species or color variations of the same animal.

There is also the debate over whether the cats actually *live* here in Vermont, or just pass through as they follow their mysterious, wide-ranging routes across the wilderness.

Certainly our state provides enough undeveloped land to allow plenty of room for catamounts. About 85 percent of Vermont is wooded. And there is no sound reason to believe big cats will not re-occupy territory where they once lived.

Another question biologists keep posing is whether the woodlands contain enough protein to support these hungry carnivores.

Admittedly, panthers can give hunters a hand in controlling the deer herd, but there's the added danger they'll develop an appetite for livestock. Several cases seem to validate this fear. An especially grisly series of attacks occurred on a remote farm in Orwell over a four-day period in late October 1991.

On a Sunday, farmer Kenneth Pope found one of his heifers with scratches and deep puncture wounds on its face. He figured it had somehow gotten loose and hurt itself—maybe on a barbed wire fence.

Then on Tuesday, he discovered four more cattle with their faces sliced to ribbons. He wasn't sure what had done it—dogs, maybe—but as an added precaution, he closed and locked the barn door that night. In spite of his security efforts, something got in through a window. The unknown intruder bypassed calves in a calf house outside the barn; it ignored the full-grown, free-roaming cattle. Instead, it went directly to an area where 4- to 9-month-old cows were tied and helpless in stalls. A week and a half earlier, these heifers had been dehorned. Maybe the interloper had been attracted by the smell of the dehorning wounds. In any event, the attacker ripped and mutilated the remaining cattle.

Pope called veterinarian Kent Anderson to examine the maimed animals, which were suffering but not dead. Dr. Anderson examined the deep parallel scratches and lacerations on their faces and noses. In some cases, he found most of the flesh had been torn away. Facial bones had been crushed into the sinuses. Whatever had done this had to be strong and weigh over 100 pounds. "I wouldn't rule out dogs," Dr. Anderson said, "but it wasn't as likely." Not likely, because of the high number of scratch wounds and the absence of bite marks anywhere but on the front of the head.

Pope and Anderson concluded a large cat was responsible for the savage mutilation of fourteen heifers and one cow, a cat far bigger than a house cat, bobcat or lynx. The notion was reinforced because the mutilated animals were left alive. Members of the cat family have a habit of playing with prey; that might explain the pattern of attacking without killing. Anderson recommended that the suffering animals be killed. This resulted in a loss of over $10,000 for Kenneth Pope.

Not long ago, the Vermont Fish and Wildlife Department steadfastly maintained there were no panthers in Vermont. Now they contend that any catamounts seen here are not descendants of the ancient Vermont panthers, but ex-pets or nomadic wanderers.

On June 2, 1994, hoping to get the final word on big cats, I interviewed Vermont State Naturalist Charles W. Johnson. Although he has never seen a catamount, he has personally observed and photographed tracks and collected hair samples. "The number of sightings is a convincing argument in favor of the cats' presence," he said, "but the lack of specimens is puzzling. Still, I don't think there's any question that they're here; the real question is whether there is a breeding population or if they're just passing through. It seems like there are too many sightings for transients . . ."

"And the black panthers," I asked. "Could people really be seeing those?"

"I investigated one of those a couple years ago," Johnson said. "If [black panthers] are here, there probably isn't any question that they're released pets. People have always been able to get them—legally or illegally. But domesticated animals are not very well equipped to survive in the wild."

When I pressed for his feeling about resident catamounts, our resident naturalist told me, "I personally believe they are here . . . It would be exciting to see the restoration of a species that was once native to the state. It would be spiritually wonderful, seeing nature restore itself like that."

Old Slipperyskin and His Kin

It can be argued that Samuel de Champlain was Vermont's first cryptozoologist, though I'm sure he never used the term. He probably never called himself a *monster hunter*, either. But when he ventured here in 1609, not only did he hear about weird aquatic creatures, but he also learned of—then immediately disregarded—tales of another Green Mountain monster.

It's a monster that is still sighted to this day. And is still disregarded just as fervently.

Encounters are not rare. They've been routinely covered by various media. Yet many Vermonters are surprised and properly incredulous to learn they are sharing the state with this particular creature.

What is it? Let's see if we can figure it out.

Perhaps the first *recorded* sighting of our mystery monster was in 1759 during the French and Indian War. Major Robert Rogers (of *Northwest Passage* fame) and his rangers were returning from their attack on the St. Francis Indians. Just south of Missisquoi Bay, Rogers and company encountered the beast. One of the rangers—a scout named Deluth—kept a journal in which he described the creature as looking like: ". . . a large black bear, who would throw large pine cones and nuts down upon us from trees and ledges . . ."

Smart bear! Yet this canny creature was no stranger to local Indians. They even had a name for it: *Wejuk*, meaning "Wet Skin."

Vermont's earliest settlers recorded many similar visits to Vermont's elusive zoo. Town histories are full of run-ins with some very odd critters. One notable example was repeatedly encountered in the townships of Morgan, Maidstone, Lemington and Victory in the late 1700s and early 1800s.

This fearsome oddity came to be known as "Old Slipperyskin." The creature was said to resemble a huge bear, but unlike any *known* bear it always walked upright, like a man. It was said to have a mean disposition, and sometimes it sought revenge against individuals who had offended it by filling their sap buckets with stones or terrifying their children. Sometimes, just for fun, it destroyed fences, tore up gardens, frightened livestock, or flattened cornfields.

Then it had a way of disappearing by carefully backtracking in its own prints, leaving a trail that ended abruptly and mysteriously.

In her *History of Lemington, Vermont* (privately published, 1976) Marion M. Daley relates:

> The story is told that an old bear once terrorized this part of the country for many years and committed wholesale destruction. He was a mean animal, and evidently had a grudge against humans. He destroyed their fences, ripped up their gardens, frightened their cows and sheep, tromped through the corn fields and caused no end of mayhem. The

> settlers came to refer to the bear as "Slipperyskin," for the reason that he managed to elude every trap that was set for him. He was a huge bear, the stories relate, and he always ran on his hind legs and never on all fours. Before a hunter could lay his gunsights on him, the old bear would vanish into the woods silent and swift as a drift of smoke. He is said to have left tracks as big as wagon wheels. His legs, in fact, were compared with spruce logs, and for what it's worth, it is told he squeezed the sap out of the maple trees when he felt inclined. For maliciousness and cunning, it was claimed he would never be compared, except to humans. He seemed to enjoy himself immensely, frightening people and livestock, kicking over manure piles and throwing stones into machinery left in fields. Where the old bear came from and why he eventually disappeared entirely is a mystery.

Mystery indeed. Or folk tale? Or maybe something else?

Around 1815, Vermont Governor Jonas Galusha promised to get rid of Old Slipperyskin once and for all. Known as an excellent hunter, the governor organized a hunting party and entered the Maidstone woods where the beast had last been seen.

Galusha—so the story goes—had covered himself with the scent of female bear. Then, gun in hand, he stalked the pesky critter alone. Shortly the governor came whooping and bellowing back into camp screaming, "Outta my way boys, I'm bringin' him back alive!"

Old Slipperyskin was in hot pursuit of Governor Galusha. The hunters scattered and no one thought to shoot.

These stories—hovering between tall tales and historical hyperbole—have enormous charm, so it's easy to overlook the fact that today we have no idea what Old Slipperyskin actually was.

The core facts seem to be these: it resembled a bear and walked like a man; it was apparently miffed because people were starting to intrude on what for centuries had been its own private domain; it was vindictive, occasionally hostile and—so it would seem—highly intelligent. But the real identity of Old Slipperyskin *may not* be lost in legend because sightings of this hairy enigma continue to this day.

Before we hazard a guess about Old Slipperyskin's identity, let's take a look at a slightly more contemporary case. What follows is typical of news stories concerning Wejuk (or Slipperyskin) that appeared with alarming regularity during the nineteenth century: On October 18, 1879 the *New York Times* ran a front-page article:

> Pownal, VT., Oct. 17—Much excitement prevailed among the sportsmen of this vicinity over the story that a wild man was seen on Friday last by two young men while hunting in the mountains south of Williamstown. The young men describe the creature as being about five feet high, resembling a man in form and movement, but covered all over with bright red hair, and having a long straggling beard, and with very wild eyes.

Wejuk. Wild Man. Old Slipperyskin. Maybe even the Bennington Monster. Today we call this formidable creature by another name; we call him Bigfoot.

The late Dr. Warren Cook of Castleton State College kept files on Bigfoot encounters for years. His records suggest that a real hot spot for Vermont Bigfoot activity is a circle roughly encompassing Hubbardton, Rutland, Poultney and Fair Haven. Route 4 runs right through the middle of this circle, connecting Rutland and Whitehall, New York. There have been so many sightings along that road that we might call it Bigfoot Boulevard.

In fact, what Cook referred to as one of the most striking Bigfoot reports of modern times occurred just across the state line, in New York. It was August 25, 1976. The witness was police officer Brian Gossellin. "Myself and one of the state troopers were out there and I was turning around in the middle of the road, and he was down the far end turning around. My headlights on my parked car picked up a pair of eyeballs—big, red eyeballs—and I turned the lights of the car off. I shined my flashlight out there and that's when I [saw] the thing look right at me.

"I called the trooper on the CB who was with me. He went into the field where I saw it. . . . Something came crashing through the woods. I turned my headlights on and it was about 30 feet in front of me . . ."

Gossellin was brave. He got out of his car to face the thing. Kneeling in firing position, he prepared to discharge his .357 revolver. But he didn't pull the trigger.

"All it did was stand there. It put its hands in front of its eyes. Hands—I don't know if that's what they were. I couldn't see any fingers. All it did was scream at the top of its lungs. I watched him for a good minute, then he turned around and started back into the woods. It went about seven and a half to eight feet tall and weighed about 400 pounds, I'd say.

"It had big red eyeballs that bulged about half an inch off his face. As far as the mouth and nose, I didn't notice any. I was too scared and shook up . . ."

Why didn't he shoot?

Gossellin explained it to Dr. Cook this way: "It was very humanlike. You would have to have been there to understand. Then I could ask you the same question."

To me, this is rather a disturbing notion: not just that there might be mysterious giant hominids in our midst, but that they might be somehow . . . human.

The sheer number of encounters is disturbing too. Giant, hairy, manlike creatures have been reported in every state except Rhode Island. Dr. Cook chronicled over 150 sightings in the Northeast, 33 in Vermont.

Of course those are the *reported* sightings. I wonder how many people see a Bigfoot and don't tell anyone simply to avoid the inevitable ridicule?

The skeptic in me asks, can so many witnesses be hallucinating?

The persistence of evidence suggests they are not.

Evidence?

• February 1951. Sudbury Swamp: Lumbermen Rowell and Kennedy return to work and discover a canvas-covered oil drum has been moved overnight. Someone, or something, had moved the 450-pound fuel drum from its place on the tractor and carried it several hundred feet toward the woods. When they checked the ground near the tractor, they found dozens of huge prints of naked feet. Rowell photographed the footprints with his Polaroid.

EVIDENCE: Pictures of humanlike footprints 20 inches long and 8 inches wide.

• Spring 1984. Chittenden: A man (who wishes to remain unidentified) is wakened by loud screaming in his dooryard. Normally, this long-time hunter isn't afraid of much, but he told investigator Ted Pratt, "I just couldn't get out of bed. It was a horrible scream. It lasted five to seven seconds." Then something even more terrifying occurred. He heard something rip his cellar door off its hinges. Whatever it was checked out his basement, then fled.

EVIDENCE: A handprint, a footprint and a broken door made of solid 2-inch oak.

• October 1976. Northeastern Rutland County: A Rutland businessman (who also won't reveal his name) was taking photographs for a land-development project. When the pictures were developed, one showed what appeared to be the upper torso and head of a gigantic Bigfoot-like creature.

Dr. Cook sent the photographic negative to a California lab for analysis. No evidence of tampering was discovered. When Cook visited the spot in question, he found no tree stump or rock formation that could account for the strange photographic phenomenon.

EVIDENCE: What might be a photograph of an actual Vermont Bigfoot.

Of course none of this evidence, nor the castings made from hundreds of footprints, can be considered conclusive. No proof can be accepted until we've found a body. Or captured a live Bigfoot. Or killed a specimen.

Sightings continue. Some of them, of course, are mistakes in perception. Some, as we have seen, are hoaxes. But the others, what of them? Assuming there really is something unknown roaming the Vermont woods, what in the world might it be?

Most likely it's one of two things: some form of primitive human who, against all odds, survived into the twentieth century; or maybe it's a highly evolved, manlike ape. Dr. Cook came to believe Bigfoot is *Australopithecus*, the first true hominid, now considered extinct; other researchers favor *Gigantopithecus*, a creature that lived in China some 500,000 years ago. Both share a family tree with man, though neither of them is, strictly speaking, human.

But there is a more mysterious side to Bigfoot's nature, a side that suggests the creature might not be natural, but rather *super*natural. Remember, the phenomenon is not just limited to Vermont. In spite of the fact that Bigfeet are known to every Indian tribe in North America, and that sightings have been documented all over the world for centuries, we have never found a body or killed or captured a single specimen.

Doesn't that seem odd? If they're real, why no bodies? No bones? No live specimens in our zoos, labs or neighborhoods? Why just enough evidence—footprints, hair, fuzzy photos—to keep us interested and to keep us guessing?

All we can say for sure is that Bigfoot is a mystery. But it might be more of a mystery than most people realize. My guess is that a hundred years from now we'll have exactly the same amount of evidence and proof we had a hundred years ago. And Bigfoot will still be running wild and unclassified amid the hills and forests of Vermont.

A Bigfoot Case Book

• April 1984. Hartland: Driving north on Interstate 91 around six a.m., within sight of the Hartland Dam, James Guyette spotted a "huge hairy animal-man" swinging its arms as it walked along the roadside about 100 yards away. It was tall and lanky, the witness reported, clearly walking upright on two legs. The creature moved down the bank beside the Interstate heading west, away from the Connecticut River. Later, when telling his wife about the encounter, Guyette started to cry.

• June 1985. Peacham: Two men were in a boat, fishing on Foster's Pond. They both saw a hairy form on the shore. At first they thought it was a bear, so they rowed closer to get a better look. The "bear" turned and ran into a cedar swamp. But there could be no mistake—the thing was running upright, on two legs. Before it disappeared they saw the light-colored soles of its feet.

• September 20, 1985. West Rutland: At about 8:30 p.m., the Davis family had a weird encounter. Sixteen-year-old Bob Davis saw a trail of footprints near Route 4A. "I started walking up the road and saw a black image. It was taller than me and ran like a human. I saw it and threw rocks at it."

Theresa Davis said, "We heard a loud thrashing noise."

Ed Davis heard grunting and screeching.

Al Davis went into the woods to investigate and discovered the creature gave off a "swampy" smell.

Examining the spot the next morning, the family found distinct tracks in the compacted gravel of the road. Dr. Warren Cook and a Rutland schoolteacher named Mr. Loomis took castings that were 14 inches long and 7 inches wide.

Winhall's Woodman

To conclude this chapter, here's one of the strangest and most perplexing things I've heard lately. Details came in a letter from a Brattleboro woman named Arlene Tarantino.

Back in the summer of 1985, Arlene managed an office for a local developer. On her day off, she grabbed a book and headed off into the Winhall woods, about 35 miles northwest of Brattleboro. It was a beautiful summer day, perfect for a hike.

At an isolated place known as Pike's Falls, she found a spot to sit and read. Then she heard something. She caught motion from the corner of her eye.

A form whipped past, moving like lightning, violently disturbing the leaves in its path. Suddenly it jumped through the bushes, landing about 15 feet away.

What she saw so short-circuited her sense of reality that in the nine years that followed, she hasn't been able to let it go. For there, standing before her, was what seemed to be a human being. His body, she says, was thin and youthful, with "muscles . . . like ropes wrapped around his skeleton." Yet his face looked old, almost ancient, with ". . . cheeks [that] were . . . wrinkled in a long thin fan of heavy creases." His gray eyes were clear and sharp, but vacant.

And he was completely naked, with straggly, ragged body hair that seemed abnormally long. His gnarled legs, she recalls, were positioned in an apelike crouch. Height was difficult to estimate because of his stooped posture, though she guesses he was about five to five and a half feet tall, weighing about 120 pounds.

She says he moved like a chimp moves, using all fours." Yet he traveled "as fast as you could imagine. . . . If you've ever seen a dog run so fast that it almost falls sideways, this is the speed [he] attained."

Fearing she'd be in danger if she moved, Arlene remained very still, eventually letting her eyes drop to the book on her lap. She doesn't remember what happened next, but she feels she may have been immobile, possibly entranced, for as much as forty minutes. When she looked up, the visitor was gone.

As a feeling of terror mounted, she got up and ran away.

Now, nearly ten years later, the encounter still affects her. She's convinced it was a human being—not a bear or a Bigfoot. In fact, she suspects he might be some kind of feral person, a lost soul who doesn't even realize he's human.

Her fear has passed. Today she looks on this stranger with compassion, convinced he has suffered greatly. She has even given him a name: Woodman.

That was to be Arlene's only meeting with Woodman. She has never seen him again, nor does she know of any other witnesses.

As for me, I hardly dare speculate about this odd encounter. My mind ticks off a number of possibilities, but they all seem so incredible I can't put them on paper.

Lake Memphremagog
Dead Creek
North Hero
Westmore
St. Albans
Grand Isle
Colchester
Lake Willoughby
Burlington
Lake Champlain
Shelburne
Woodbury Lake
Vergennes
Ascutney

Here Monsters Dwell

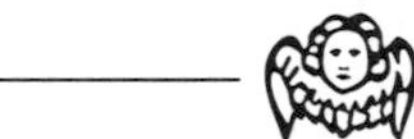

On a sunny Saturday—August 29, 1981—the manicured grounds at Shelburne Farms were teeming with monster hunters. Scientists and interested laypersons from all over the country had gathered to participate in a seminar.

The topic: Does Champ Exist?

This forum brought eyewitnesses and skeptics together, perhaps for the first time in such great numbers. From nine in the morning to four in the afternoon, everyone tried to solve Vermont's greatest and most enduring mystery.

J. Richard Greenwall of the University of Texas was there. He is a co-founder of the International Society of Cryptozoology. Co-founder, author and noted monster hunter Dr. Roy Mackal was there from the University of Chicago. Dr. George Zug of the Smithsonian Institution was there too.

The kickoff speaker, UVM's William Eddy, put the mystery in an interesting perspective. He said the question is not "Does Champ exist?" but rather "Can Champ exist?"

And the answer is "Yes."

The conditions in Lake Champlain are perfect for supporting a breeding population of Champ creatures, a population large enough to have sustained the species—whatever it may be—for, presumably, thousands of years.

The surge of national interest that led directly to the Shelburne Farms conference followed the release of what is arguably the single most compelling piece of evidence supporting Champ's existence—the so-called Mansi photograph.

In June 1981, the photograph was released to the media. In response, Lake Champlain suddenly became known as America's Loch Ness. Since then, Champ has become a celebrity, appearing in newspapers and magazines all over the world. Together with Sandra Mansi, Champ made his network TV debut in 1993. They appeared before millions of viewers in the hit NBC show "Unsolved Mysteries."

The Monster Hunter

THE HIGHLIGHT OF THE 1981 CONFERENCE was Joseph W. Zarzynski, founder and head of the Lake Champlain Phenomena Investigation Group. As I listened in wonder, Zarzynski spoke about the history of Champ sightings and about his own investigations. Even then, it occurred to me that Zarzynski was something of a romantic character, a dreamer who'd spent years in the wilds looking for dragons. In fact, I thought, he might well be the hero of a novel. I had no way of knowing that in the decade to follow, our paths were to cross a number of times.

Several years after the conference, when I began researching my novel based on Champ, *Dark Twilight*, I realized that my protagonist had a real-life counterpart. Somewhat timidly, not sure what to expect, I sought out Zarzynski and asked him to help with background material for my book.

He was nearly as fascinating as Champ. His attraction to the Lake Champlain Monster began in the mid-'70s. Since then, he has logged more hours than anyone else trying to prove the monster's existence. With tremendous singleness of purpose, he has spent summer after summer and tens of thousands of his own dollars in a twenty-year monster hunt that has disclosed far more about human optimism and endurance than it has about sea serpents.

But Zarzynski knows Champ *can* exist.

And if it exists, he wants to prove it.

Since 1974, Zarzynski has been a respected member of the faculty at Saratoga Springs Junior High School. He's also an underwater archaeologist who has personally discovered wrecks from the French and Indian War—rare historical finds of national importance.

Now in his mid-40s, Zarr (as he likes to be called) stands six-foot five. He's an accomplished runner, swimmer and diver, all useful skills for finding—or perhaps escaping—water monsters.

With the help of his wife, Pat Meaney, Zarr's Lake Champlain Phenomena Investigation Group has catalogued well over 300 monster sightings dating back to 1609. He publishes "Champ Channels," an occasional newsletter devoted to monster lore, and has authored two books, *Champ, Beyond the Legend* (the definitive work on the subject) and *Monster Wrecks of Loch Ness and Lake Champlain.* Zarr is considered the foremost authority on the elusive Lake Champlain creature (he never refers to it as a monster; he prefers "Champ Creature" or USO: Unidentified Swimming Object). His careful research has won endorsements from such diverse sources as Dr. George Zug of the Smithsonian Institution and the best-selling novelist Clive Cussler.

Thanks largely to Zarzynski's efforts, *Belua aquatica champlainiensis*, the Champ creatures, are protected by the legislatures of New York and Vermont.

I thought it might be interesting to let this real life monster hunter tell us about Champ. The following is an abbreviated transcript from a recorded interview with Joseph W. Zarzynski, taped in the fall of 1991:

CITRO: *Tell me how you got interested in tracking the Lake Champlain monster? What got you started?*

ZARZYNSKI: It goes back to my interest in the Loch Ness monster, something that has interested me since I was a child. A friend of mine, a lifelong resident of this area, said, "You know, if you're interested in the Loch Ness monster, what about the Lake Champlain monster?" I thought he was pulling my leg, but he really wasn't. So I started to investigate and found out that indeed there was an abundance of reported sightings, almost right in my own backyard.

Do you think the two monsters and the two lakes have anything in common?

It's uncanny. I think that's probably the best word to describe the similarities between the two bodies of water and the reported sightings. Both lakes are fresh water, they're both deep, they both have an abundance of fish life. Both were formed roughly eight to ten thousand years ago as fresh water. Prior to that, they had marine influence because they were extensions of the North Atlantic. They're both in that realm of 40 to 60 degrees north and south latitude—within that band Dr. Roy Mackal likes to call "the lake monster band."

In terms of the sightings, I think we're talking about creatures that are probably the same species. Large, dark in color, head that looks like that of a horse, a snake or a dog. And possibly two or four flippers. Although I'd have to say that when you look at the sightings from Loch Ness compared to Lake Champlain, some of the Loch Ness witnesses are talking about a real big water bull, something 60 to 70 feet in length! We just don't see that in Lake Champlain. Apparently the Champ creatures are a little smaller.

Tell me a little about the history of the Champ sightings. How many have there been?

There have been over three hundred since 1609. Some people believe the first recorded sighting was made in 1609 by the famous French explorer Samuel de Champlain. One account says he saw a large fish, probably not a Champ, but a lake sturgeon or garpike. Another historian, Marjorie Porter, wrote that Champlain actually saw a monster 20 feet long, with a head like a horse, and as wide as a barrel. So, Champlain's sighting is controversial. The next sighting was in 1819 with a few dozen more recorded in the nineteenth century. So you can see we're dealing with a phenomenon that was not just created in the last half of this century, while Nessie (the Loch Ness Monster) was becoming so popular.

What, in your opinion, is the single most dramatic, or perhaps most convincing, Champ sighting?

That's a tough question. I'd say the most dramatic sighting was by Sandra and Tony Mansi in 1977. During that sighting they actually photographed Champ . . . or what they claimed was Champ. In many respects, it reminds me of the 1934 photo taken at Loch Ness, by Dr. Wilson. Both depict a dark creature with head and neck projected out of the water.

[*Author's Note:* Sadly, according to a March 1994 disclosure, Loch Ness researchers Alastair Boyd and David Martin revealed that the so-called "Surgeon's Photo" was a hoax. They maintain that Dr. Wilson, an eminent London gynecologist, was one of four conspirators who concocted the hoax. Allegedly, the last surviving conspirator, Christian Spurling, confessed on his death bed that he had constructed the model Dr. Wilson photographed.]

I've heard a lot of critical, or at least skeptical, stuff about the Mansi photo. What about that?

Oh sure. It's got its positive and its negative sides. It's the classic photograph of Champ, if for no other reason than the amount of publicity it's had. But when you start to investigate, you see that there are some shortcomings. It was taken in early July of 1977. It wasn't until two years later that the family came out of the closet and started to talk about the photograph. At that time, in 1979, we tried to take the family up to the location, the exact location, and we couldn't find it! They were a little bit disoriented. But to their credit, things *had* changed. What was once a field was now condos and houses. Dirt roads had been paved. In two to three years there'd been a general facelift. The other problem, which is major, is that they couldn't produce the negative. The family apparently tossed the negative out or misplaced it. So we're dealing with a purported lake monster photograph, a place we couldn't find and no negative. The photo did go through a series of tests out at the University of Arizona, and we still believe it's the classic photo.

Yet for all the finger-pointing that has gone on, the Mansis were probably the most down-to-earth, normal people that you could find. One thing that helped convince me was that after they had the photograph developed, they pinned it up on their kitchen wall. What is more normal than that? They pinned it on their kitchen wall and there it sat.

So who were some of the other "credible" witnesses?

Several actually stand out. There was one man, I forget his name now. He lived on the lake in a houseboat. He was probably the most nautical-minded witness. When he talked about his sighting, it was so many points to the port side. He referenced the compass, and things like this.

Then there was another guy—I think his name was Morse—who had a land sighting. That's really rare.

You are considered the expert on the Lake Champlain creature. More than anyone else, you've weighed all the pros and cons. So level with me, in your heart of hearts do you really believe there is something unknown in Lake Champlain?

Yes I do. However—and this is the first time I've ever admitted this in an interview—I'm beginning to wonder if we'll ever conclusively prove Champ's existence. I used to be 99.9 percent sure Champ existed. Now I'm down to 95 percent. Why? I suppose it's the seventeen years of effort, with little to show but three hundred Champ sightings, a few photos, and some rather poor video. Nonetheless, the challenge is still there and I suppose that's what drives me. The excitement of planning expeditions, the thrill when field work techniques work, and the people . . . I've met such fascinating people in the search. . . .

And the thing that really excites me and regenerates me—the battery charge—is that new sighting. I go and I talk to the people. I look in their eyes and I see this blast of energy that sort of comes out of their eyes and their mouths and it hits me and it just keeps me going.

Yet you've never seen the monster yourself?

But I have! In August 1988, my wife, several people and myself saw what could have been Champ, or . . .

Tell me about it.

It was almost a surrealistic experience simply because I was trying to do more than one thing at a time. We had a 63-foot air-sea rescue boat that was on loan to us for helping train a bunch of Sea Scouts. Part of our work involved doing side-scan sonar near Westport, New York. There was Marty Klein of Klein Associates whose company developed the sonar. He'd done a lot of work in the '70s at Loch Ness. And my wife, Pat. They were sitting down enjoying a very hot sunny day at the stern of this huge, militarylike vessel.

The rest of the group was focused on the sonar unit. Pat and Marty were the first to observe this dark thing in the water. We'd just made a turn toward the New York side. They said, "We see something out there." When I looked, all I initially saw was the dark wave that had been created by our turn. But what they were talking about was something much further beyond us. When they got me away from the equipment, I looked through the binoculars and could clearly see something very animate. It was dark in color, and it was coming out of the water. The expression that my wife and I used at the time really stuck—it was *thrashing* on the surface. It would just thrash. It was heading toward the Vermont side at a range of maybe half a mile to a mile. I didn't see a head, but it was definitely animate. It could have been a fish porpoising or something like that. But there was some size to it. I could see a 3- to 4-foot length of something, and that was only part of it. It was not just a disturbance of the water; it was definitely animate. The interesting phenomenon was that we had three trained observers and still in our minds we were saying, "Is it this? Or is it this? Or this?" I took quite a few minutes to say there was something definitely out there.

If there really are Champ animals out there, then there would have to be a breeding pool large enough to account for sightings dating back to before Europeans settled here. How many Champ animals would be required?

I believe we're dealing with a community of twelve to twenty-five individuals. I think the lake would support a colony of that many.

So with that many, how come Champ animals aren't spotted more frequently? And how come a dead body has never shown up?

Well, we must realize Champ's domain is subsurface. So to find it, we must think subsurface. We'll find a body if we look long and hard enough in the deep waters, 150 feet and deeper. That's where they live and die.

But don't you think it's odd that no remains have ever been found? Of all the reported monsters in Lake Champlain and Loch Ness, and after so many years of sightings, there's still not even a carcass?

I think its very odd. That's why in the last few years, we've tried to put a little high-tech into it to find a carcass.

Over the last several years, my LCPI [Lake Champlain Phenomena Investigation] has used a Klein side-scan sonar and a Minirover Mark II ROV [Remotely Operated Vehicle] to look for a Champ carcass on videotape.

In spite of all your effort and all the evidence, I can't help but guess a lot of people must think you're a crackpot, right?

Oh yeah, sure. It doesn't bother me because I firmly believe that if those same people were objective enough to sit down and look at the piecemeal evidence and assemble it as a cryptozoological jigsaw puzzle, they would come away at least saying there must be something there. People *are* seeing something, but what are they seeing? I think the lofty goal of wanting to know the truth may even superimpose itself over finding Champ. I just want to know what's there.

You know, we really lost something when author and cryptozoologist Tim Dinsdale died. If you read his writing you'll see he really captures the essence of what monster hunting was all about. He puts monster hunting in a very noble light. He says, "The truth is a cloth of gold." You're not just looking for a monster, you're trying to find something much more important—the truth.

I'd like to conclude with this question: If you do find Champ, then he'll become just another page in a zoology text along with mountain gorillas and leather-backed turtles. So if you find him, what then? Where does that leave you?

For me, there always will be great mysteries out there. Lake Champlain is simply one of the great mysteries, one of the Mount Everests. There will be another tall peak or another low valley. But I have a feeling that this one, Champ, will be around for a while.

I'm just hoping that myself and others are doing a proper job inspiring younger people to come along and pick up the search. This is a key thing for the cryptozoological community: to insure that this knowledge, training and experience is passed along to other people. When the baton is passed to a new generation, I hope they'll have the knowledge and interest to continue.

THE HUNT

AMONG THAT NEW GENERATION OF MONSTER HUNTERS, we might include Dennis Hall of Vergennes. In 1985, Hall videotaped a moving figure that he believes to be Champ. Additionally, Hall might well hold the record for Champ sightings: he claims fifteen in the last twenty years. Which might make him something of an expert.

In that capacity, Hall participated in the largest and most generously funded monster hunt in the history of Lake Champlain. From July 21 to September 10, 1993, a film crew from the Tokyo Broadcasting System was in Vermont preparing a ninety-minute documentary on Champ for Japanese television.

Fifteen boats equipped with hundreds of thousands of dollars' worth of electronic equipment combed the lake. The search involved aerial surveillance by helicopter and a twenty-four-hour videotaping of a section of lake where, theoretically, Champ would eventually surface.

But, as usual, Champ proved a wily beast and never showed up for the photographers.

Luckily, the crew didn't have to return to Japan empty-handed, thanks to Jim Hotaling of Willsboro, New York. Hotaling used a paper graph to record underwater images detected by sonar. Most were unremarkable: a good-sized salmon, a school of fish. But then the sonar sighted something interesting: a large irregular mass, 20 feet long, moving in 60 feet of water.

Hotaling was stumped. "I don't know if it's Champ," he said. "It's abnormal in shape. Very dense. I've never seen anything like it before."

CHAMP SCRAPBOOK

FOR A MOMENT, let's assume Champ is not some sort of hallucination or supernatural beast. Okay, then what is it? The most credible theory is that it's a dinosaur, some sort of surviving prehistoric animal. Certainly there is evidence that Champ was around in prehistoric times. The Abenaki spoke of the *tatoskok*, a creature as large as a tree with a head like a horse's but with horns. They observed how it roiled the water, reminiscent of Zarzynski's sighting, where he described Champ "thrashing" on the surface.

A lingering legend claims the Indians presented Samuel de Champlain with the monster's head. Of course the relic has long since disappeared, so we don't know, but one of today's theories holds that Champlain was actually given the head of a monstrous sturgeon.

Many articles say that Champlain logged a monster sighting in his journals. In *Vermont Life* Magazine's Summer 1970 issue, historian Marjorie L. Porter wrote that Champlain "recorded his impression of a serpent-like creature about twenty feet long, as thick as a barrel and with the head of a horse." Exactly why Ms. Porter reported a serpent twenty feet long will probably never be known. She has passed away, and the *Vermont Life* article doesn't list sources. Another questionable quotation often attributed to Champlain's journals has him witnessing "a great long monster, lying in the lake, allowing birds to land on its beak, then snapping them in whole." He does say something like this, but he makes it clear he is repeating Indian legend.

Historian and monster hunter Jacques Boisvert of Magog, Quebec, has a different interpretation. "In fact, what he saw," Boisvert maintains, "was a fish named *Chaousarou* by the Indians." As a schoolboy in Quebec, Boisvert had studied Champlain's journals in the original French. He says, "If Champlain had seen a sea serpent I would have known . . ."

According to the source material, *The Works of Samuel de Champlain* (edited by H.P. Biggar), Champlain said he saw some

"Chaousarou" about "five feet long, which were as big as my thigh, and had a head as large as my two fists, with a snout two feet and a half long, and a double row of very sharp, dangerous teeth."

A *Chaousarou*, Boisvert explains, "is a fish in the family of the *Lepisosteus osseus*." We call it a longnose gar, garpike, or simply, gar. While this debate may take some of the proverbial wind out of Champ's metaphorical sails, let's not forget that the gar is an ancient animal. It is one of three "old age fish" known to have inhabited Lake Champlain since prehistoric times. The sturgeon, the bowfin and the longnose gar have survived ecological adaptation and continue to live in Lake Champlain today, just as they did millennia ago.

So if they can survive, why not Champ?

Over the years, scads of credible and unambiguous sightings build a very strong case. In fact, one wonders why Champ's existence has to be proved over and over, year after year. There are over 300 reported sightings. These translate into a staggering number of individual witnesses.

There have been land sightings, water sightings, and Christine Breyetter even spotted Champ from the air back in 1973 when she was flying over Lake Champlain in her father's airplane.

Add to these accounts all the sightings that have gone unreported and we're no doubt into the thousands.

One wonders why, if it takes but a single witness to put someone in jail, hundreds of witnesses can't establish Champ's reality? And if a jury of twelve can convince a judge, how many eyewitnesses does it take to convince a skeptic?

Of course there is no way I can chronicle all the Champ sightings since Champlain met the *Chaousarou*, but the following scrapbook highlights some of the more curious, and the more convincing.

Multiple-Witness Sightings

CHAMPLAIN'S ACCOUNT, like the account of most any individual, may be questionable. But once in a while, there occurs a Champ sighting so compelling, so convincing, that we are forced *not* to set the legend aside and forget it.

I'm talking about multiple-witness sightings, when many people report exactly the same thing. These mass sightings are impossible to dismiss. And over the years, there have been a lot of them.

• In July 1870, everyone on a steamship excursion saw the monster near Charlotte, Vermont. The name of the vessel is lost, but the story of the startling event lingers like a ghost.

• The following August 31, the *Temperance Advocate* of St. Albans reported, "The What Is It of Lake Champlain was again interviewed near Barber's Point on Monday last. It was in full view of passengers of steamer *Curlew*, and was an object projecting some distance from the water and going at railroad speed."

• In July 1873, the crew and passengers of the steamer *W.B. Eddy* watched the monster near Dresden, New York.

• 1892: Captain Moses Blow had worked for the Champlain Transportation Company for forty-two years, with twenty-eight of them on Lake Champlain. One serene summer day, he was piloting the *A. Williams* when he, his crew and some passengers got a good look at the serpent. It was early afternoon, some two and a half miles north of Basin Harbor. Blow's daughter gives more details: "They were at anchor and all of a sudden the boat started rocking, and they couldn't imagine what in the world was the matter and they're looking all around when all of a sudden, the head, then the neck came out of the water and it looked right straight at them, and then he [Captain Blow] said, 'Let's get out of here,' and then they headed for Burlington. . . ."

The boat was at anchor because, coincidentally, a group of scientists was aboard to check the depth of the lake. They measured to 400 feet and didn't reach bottom. The temperature down there was 38 degrees. The scientists told Captain Blow that if anyone drowned there, they would never come up—the pressure would hold the body in place.

A sad footnote to the story may illustrate why no Champ carcass has ever been found. Apparently, Captain Blow's brother Charlie and nephew Harvey later drowned at that exact spot—and their bodies never surfaced.

• April 1915: the *Burlington News*: "The Lake Champlain sea serpent . . . was seen at the 1892 encampment of the American Canoe Association when, coming to the surface in the neighborhood of a flotilla of cruising canoes, he scattered the occupants in panic."

• And as recently as 1945, people aboard the *S. S. Ticonderoga* observed the monster cavorting somewhere near the middle of the lake.

• July 8, 1983: Laura Coble, a counselor at South Hero's Camp Greylock, reported that ten counselors and twenty-five children saw Champ's humps as it swam past on the lake.

• Then, on July 30, 1984, the largest mass Champ sighting in history occurred aboard a sightseeing boat called *The Spirit of Ethan Allen*.

It was near Appletree Point, just outside Burlington. A private party was in progress, celebrating the wedding anniversary of a Massachusetts couple. The time: about six o'clock in the evening. Between seventy and eighty-six passengers were aboard.

The boat's owner, Michael Shea, is a professional airplane pilot and a keen observer—maybe that's why he was the first to spot something unusual.

"It was a perfect flat calm day on the lake," he told me. "Not a ripple on the water. . . . I saw it about 200 feet . . . away. . . . First I thought it was a stray wake. . . . I stared at it awhile and noticed [whatever it was] was creating its own wake."

By the time he climbed to the upper deck, the band had stopped playing. People were rushing to the rails to watch the humped creature swimming beside the boat. Many out-of-staters had never heard of The Lake Champlain Monster, but they were all seeing . . . something.

Even the Captain saw it. And, according to Mike, "He was one of those hard people to convince of anything."

Another witness, Bette Morris of Grand Isle—daughter of the anniversary couple—anticipated the skeptic's argument and said, "We hadn't been drinking all that much at the time, either."

The creature remained for about three minutes. Shea said three to five humps had surfaced, each about 12 inches out of the water. He estimated the creature was about 30 feet long. It was ". . . green-brown [and] slimy-looking like a frog," he said. It swam parallel with the boat for 1,000 yards until a speedboat approached. Then the creature turned 90 degrees and submerged.

Mike recalls the image vividly: "You know how when something goes underwater it turns sort of a yellowish color? Especially in this water. I could see that. It disappeared and the wake stopped."

Astonishingly, several people saw the creature reappear about fifteen minutes later!

Bette Morris snapped a picture, but like so many Champ photographs, the image proved inconclusive.

Today Mike's father, Captain Frank Shea, drives the boat. He's a proud Vermonter with a contagious love for the lake and its history. Since the 1984 sighting, twenty to twenty-five people have stopped by to tell him they were part of that memorable cruise. Captain Shea says, "They always tell me exactly the same story: the color, how it turned, what it did—with this exception: they differ in the length; some say it's 30 feet long, some say it's 100, some say 75."

In spite of his seven years on the lake, Captain Shea has never had a definite sighting. "I have personally seen water disturbances many, many times," he says, "but I've never seen a head or a definite form or anything like that."

But he has repeatedly seen mysterious splashing that he cannot explain. "Mostly it's something more than just a fish. I know what a fish splashing is like . . . but this is something larger."

Even though this is considered the largest mass-sighting in history, Mike Shea is careful about how much he'll admit to. "I'll never say it was Champ," he told me. "If you heard me, I didn't say I saw Champ. I'll tell you what I saw. If you want to call it Champ, okay."

Landing Champ

In the same way we humans occasionally take to the water, Champ occasionally takes to the land. Or so it would seem. Rumors of land sightings have circulated throughout the Champlain Valley for years. Some have been documented, and these are the rarest and most unusual sightings of all.

Land sightings are of particular interest because animals spotted on the ground are not as easily misperceived as semi-submerged objects obscured by tossing waves or distorted by glaring sunshine. Imagine yourself behind the wheel, cruising down some lonely lakeside drive at twilight. Suddenly you see a 30-foot serpent dragging itself across the road in front of your car!

Impossible? Not according to Thomas E. Morse of Westport, New York, who reported just such a confrontation. It happened in 1961 while he was driving beside North West Bay. In a letter to Joseph Zarzynski, Mr. Morse said, "When first seen it appeared as a massive gunmetal gray approx. 18-inch-wide cable on the shore and out into the lake. . . . It appeared to be a monstrous eel with white teeth that raked rearward in the mouth." Mr. Morse said that while on shore, Champ raised his head a full 4 feet. Possibly it was reacting to the sound of the car.

What may be the *oldest* reported land sighting occurred in mid-July of 1873. Animals were missing from Dresden (New York) farms. Marks on the ground suggested something had dragged them into the lake. One young farmer spotted a sizable serpent in a lakeside marsh. It was holding something in its mouth that looked like a turtle. The farmer shot at the creature, and it vanished into the water.

Around 1886, a St. Albans man was duck hunting beside the Missisquoi River (which flows into Lake Champlain). There he saw an "enormous serpent coiled up on the swampy shore and asleep . . . as large around as a man's thigh." Simply by shouldering his shotgun, he made enough noise to awaken the creature and scare it away.

At roughly the same time, the *Plattsburgh Morning Telegram* reported that, "The sea serpent . . . has left the lake and is making his way overland in the direction of Lake George. He was seen last night about five o'clock by a farmer driving to his barn with a load of hay." He saw it ". . . not five rods behind him, gliding along like a snake with its head raised about four feet from the ground . . . an immense monster anywhere from 25 to 75 feet in length. . . ."

Another interesting sighting occurred in September 1894. The *Essex County Republican* reported that four men saw "the Champlain Sea Serpent"—as Champ was then called—at Cumberland Head, near Plattsburgh, New York. "It caused a great commotion in the water . . . and came toward the shore and out of the water six feet or more upon the land."

The *Burlington News* of April 1915 told how "several observers" had spotted Champ on land. "When first sighted through a field glass, the serpent, said to be about forty feet long, was apparently stranded on a reef at the entrance to Bulwagga Bay near the Crown Point fortifications. Presently he released himself and, after a few wild plunges which lashed the water into foam, he headed for the Vermont shore in great semi-circular sweeps, finally shrinking submarine-fashion, leaving a wake which was well defined on the glassy surface of the lake."

So why did Champ slither up onto that reef in the first place?

And why, in general, does Champ crawl out of the lake at all?

In his book, *Champ: Beyond the Legend*, Zarzynski says, "One hypothesis . . . is that [the Champ creatures] are mammals, and thus have amphibious tendencies. Their land sojourns may somehow be associated with hereditary impulse 'since all known aquatic mammals are derived from land-dwelling forms.'" (This according to Dr. Roy P. Mackal's book *Searching for Hidden Animals.*)

Maybe so, maybe not. But as I study these accounts, one thing seems obvious: the monster seen on land is very different from the monster seen in water. On land, the creatures are consistently described as looking like serpents. That's quite unlike the long-necked, thick-bodied plesiosaur-like creature that most witnesses see swimming in the lake.

Does the Champ creature alter its shape when it comes on land? Do Champ creatures change as they mature, like pollywogs turning into frogs? Or are there two different varieties of "monster" in Lake Champlain? Perhaps the next generation of monster hunters will find out for sure.

The Rarest of the Rare

DURING CHAMP'S FIRST BRUSH WITH STARDOM in the early 1800s, waves of tourists flooded Lake Champlain in response to showman P.T. Barnum's offer of $50,000 for the creature—dead or alive.

As far as we know the money is unclaimed.

But there are the stories . . .

• Around 1900, Henry Washburn of Colchester was fishing in Malletts Bay with his son Carl. When Carl spotted what he thought was the monster, Henry rowed for shore, fearing the beast would overturn the boat. Years later, recalling the incident, Carl was reminded of another serpent that had been caught and tied up near North Beach in Burlington—but it had escaped without being photographed.

• Another example is more recent. In 1945, a Burlington paper reported "Baby Sea Serpent Taken in Vermont Waters—May Be Offspring of Lake Monster." The article says that Erwin Bell, an employee of the Champlain Transportation Company, captured a 14-inch reptile in Shelburne Harbor. Some people speculated that it was a young Champ animal. Others said it was some variety of fish or salamander.

In either event, the specimen seems to have disappeared.

Isn't it maddening to speculate that proof of Champ's existence might be preserved in a laboratory bottle and packed away in a forgotten crate in some attic, museum or warehouse?

The Granite Monster

And this brings us back to the subject of monster hunting. In addition to scanning the lake's surface with binoculars and camera, or probing the depths with sonar and remotely operated vehicles, Joe Zarzynski tries to prove Champ's existence in various other ways. Interviewing eyewitnesses, viewing videotapes and examining photographs are other phases of the hunt.

But proof requires something tangible, ideally a living creature or the remains of a dead one. To that end, Zarzynski occasionally gets to investigate the possibility that physical remains of a Champ creature have already been found. This kind of detective work requires following up on rumors and intriguing articles in ancient newspapers, like those cited above.

In addition to the baby Champ story, another tantalizing lead came to Zarzynski's attention in 1986. It was an article from the *Middlebury Register* of May 27, 1881:

"The proprietors of the Champlain Granite Works, located near Barn Rock Bay on Lake Champlain, claim to have discovered a petrified sea serpent of mammoth proportions, being 8 inches in diameter and nearly 50 feet long. The surface of this stone bears evidence of the outer skin of a large serpent while the inner surface shows the entrails. The proprietors are intending soon to begin excavations along the place where it lies imbedded in the dirt and granite, to ascertain its size."

Zarzynski was fascinated by this reference. After all, if a 50-foot fossilized Champ existed in 1881, it must still be around! Immediately he began an archival monster hunt that would last more than three years. By pouring over old newspapers and by visiting lakeside historical societies, Zarzynski pieced together the fascinating saga of the Granite Monster.

In the summer of 1879, Vermont-based geologist H.H. Burge discovered a supply of valuable "Labrador granite" near Barn Rock on the New York shore. He formed the Champlain Granite Company in Vergennes and purchased the site. By the spring of 1881, quarrying had begun. Shortly thereafter, workers discovered the fossilized monster in a limestone deposit.

In a June 8, 1882 edition of the *Elizabeth Town Post and Gazette*, Zarzynski found more information in an article called "An Ancient Monster." Its author had personally examined the fossil.

"Some portions were 6 inches long and some were 15 or more. The pieces were placed together and fitted so nicely there could be no room to doubt of their having been broken apart. . . . The entrails were petrified, but much darker . . . differing from the flesh part. The vertebra was visible at each broken end, and the flesh part showed traces of . . . veins." The complete fossil measured over 60 feet. Its weight was estimated at several tons.

In the University of Vermont Special Collections, Zarzynski discovered a pamphlet proving that the remarkable fossil had been exhibited in the Vergennes Town Hall during October of 1886.

And there the story ends. Zarzynski could find no trace of the fossil after the October exhibition.

So where did it go?

Champlain Valley historian Morris F. Glenn offers one theory. He recalls P.T. Barnum's interest in the Lake Champlain monster and theorizes that the legendary collector and showman might have purchased the relic for his museum of oddities.

In 1989, one of Zarzynski's colleagues searched the records at the New York Historical Society's Barnum Collection. But he found nothing about the Granite Monster.

So Vergennes is where the Granite Monster's trail comes to an end. Mr. Burge's discovery remains an enigmatic puzzle.

What could it have been? Was it Champ's fossilized great-grandfather? Or was it proof of some new species as yet unknown to science?

If the answer isn't packed away in a series of dusty wooden crates somewhere, it may well be displayed in the masonry of an unknown collector's fireplace or foundation.

Skeptic's Corner

IN AN EFFORT TO BE AN EQUAL OPPORTUNITY WRITER, I want to devote a little space to the possibility that there is no monster in Lake Champlain.

Okay, so if Champ *isn't* out there, why do people keep seeing him?

Most skeptics claim that three possibilities will explain away *all* Champ sightings:

1. HOAX—the work of generation after generation of organized and unorganized tricksters.

2. ILLUSION—seeing things. Hallucinations. Some people claim that big lakes, like the sea, "can play strange tricks on a man."

3. MISTAKE—honest misinterpretation of something already known, like tree stumps, flocks of birds, floating debris, dogs—even swimmers! Many people see a line of sturgeon or carp "porpoising," that is, breaking the surface of the water one after another, then diving again, appearing to be the monster's humps. Otters swimming single file can appear to be a long, humped body. And those who've been lucky enough to see deer dog-paddling between islands have witnessed a sight they'll never forget, no matter what they thought they saw.

So we could conceivably have three different witnesses: one playing a trick, another experimenting with hallucinogens, and a third watching a family of otters.

Three sightings and no monster.

One recurring theme in Champ sightings is *size*. People report seeing something awfully big. In such cases, sturgeon are the most likely culprits. It's probably the oldest fish in Lake Champlain, so it could account for sightings all the way back to prehistoric times. Lake Champlain sturgeon have a lifespan of about 125 years. They can grow to 7 and more feet long and weigh over 100 pounds.

In 1974, on a beach in North Hero, a sturgeon was found that weighed 130 pounds and measured 9 feet!

On June 22, 1947, Milton resident Cliff Lamphear and his son netted a sturgeon near Grand Isle. It reportedly weighed 165 to 175 pounds. And far bigger specimens have been recorded in other lakes. So who can guess the size of the never-hooked or never-netted lunkers swimming between New York and Vermont?

In a sense, there's nothing strange about sturgeon, even when they're giants. But maybe there *are* strange things in the lake. To me, one of the most interesting possible misperceptions is almost as thrilling as a real Champ sighting.

This theory was put forth by cryptozoologist Loren Coleman in a 1987 edition of "Champ Channels," Joe Zarzynski's newsletter devoted to Lake Champlain phenomena. It came as a big surprise to me to discover that *live seals* have been spotted in Lake Champlain.

I'm talking about the common harbor seal, the one we see in aquariums or along the East coast. These seals can be 4 to 6 feet long and weigh anywhere from 100 to more than 300 pounds.

The *Plattsburgh Sentinel* was probably the first to equate Champ sightings and harbor seals. In 1894, they wrote, "[There really is] a living monster of some kind . . . we have never questioned the substantial accuracy of the numerous accounts. . . . That it is a species of serpent does not follow. It may be more of the nature of a seal or sea-lion."

R.M. Anderson, in a 1946 *Bulletin of the National Museum of Canada*, said harbor seals have made their way up the St. Lawrence River and have been seen in Lake Ontario and, closer to home, in Montreal. So why not Lake Champlain?

Zadock Thompson's 1842 *History of Vermont* described an incident that took place near Burlington in 1810: "While several persons were skating upon Lake Champlain . . . they discovered a living seal . . . which had found its way through a crack and was crawling upon the ice. They took off their skates, with which they attacked and killed it. . . ." (This may give us some idea why Champ chooses to remain so elusive.)

In *Mammals of Vermont*, George L. Kirk said in 1916 that the harbor seal has been found in or near Lake Champlain three times: Burlington in 1810 and 1846, and Otter Creek in 1876. He goes on to say one is preserved in the state collection in Montpelier and another at the University of Vermont's museum. (Though this assertion may have been true at the time, I learned through a series of phone calls that the Vermont Historical Society's Museum no longer has its specimen, and UVM's seal is now in the hands of a private collector.)

In any event, these are not recent sightings. Does that mean seals are *not* being spotted in Lake Champlain anymore?

Not necessarily. Maybe they're being spotted but reported as sightings of the Lake Champlain Monster. After all, bigger perceptual blunders have been made on the lake. The biggest probably occurred on October 13, 1773, when British warships fired on what they thought was an American vessel. It turned out to be an island. To commemorate the monumental misperception forever, the island was dubbed "Carlton's Prize" in honor of the visually confused British general who opened fire.

So we have come full circle, all the way back to the skeptics' assertion: hoax, illusion or mistake.

Personally, I like to think there's a forth explanation: REALITY!

THE ALIEN AQUARIUM

I HAVE LIVED NEAR LAKE CHAMPLAIN for more than twenty years, and believe me, it's like living next door to a haunted house. I mean, just about everyone says there's a monster out there. And I've never been one to argue with so many people.

But Champ is by no means Vermont's only water monster. In fact, there are so many that the only safe place to swim might be your neighbor's pool.

Dead Creek

ANOTHER OF VERMONT'S LESS FAMILIAR AQUATIC ANOMALIES is the Serpent of Dead Creek, first reported in a 1909 issue of the *Swanton Courier*. It accosted three fishermen out for bull pout. The beast ". . . big around as a sugar barrel," scared them out of their rowboat and chased them up a tree. "It was the tallest tree in the marsh," one of them said, "but it wasn't tall enough by a hundred, maybe two hundred feet."

They described the monster this way: "The top of the head was black and hairy and shaded down to the ears to a dirty moss green." It had "shiny gray scales about the size of a baseball on the throat, with big ones down towards the belly. When it opened its terrible mouth we could see several rows of glittering white teeth ten inches long. . . . And it stuck its head out of the water . . . and sniffed a good deal like a bird dog." Of course many people suspect it was smelling something fishy . . .

The Connecticut Whatsit

EVEN SOME OF OUR RIVERS SEEM TO HAVE RESIDENT ODDITIES. For example, what are we to make of a 1968 story from United Press International, datelined Ascutney? It tells how Douglas and Dorothy Gove of Manchester, New Hampshire, were canoeing down the Connecticut River from Ryegate to Brattleboro. En route, they spied a small animal with bright green scales swimming beside them. It was between 18 and 24 inches long, and they agreed it probably weighed about 2 pounds. Eventually they watched the creature vanish beneath a tree stump on the river bank, leaving tracks and markings from its tail. The curious couple reported the incident to authorities at the state park in Ascutney, but no one could identify the tracks or recognize the reptilian creature that made them.

Woodbury Lake

THEN THERE'S THE EQUALLY ELUSIVE Woodbury Water Witch. In their winter 1975 issue, *Vermont Life* Magazine reported that "this reclusive amphibian, whose length has been estimated at anywhere up to 12 feet, generally lurks half-submerged in . . . quiet parts of . . . Woodbury Lake. While precise descriptions vary, a number of sightseers agree the Water Witch has a scaly body, a web-like tail and sports a forklike antenna . . . just above two large recessed eyes."

At least I *think* that's what *Vermont Life* said. It was a little difficult to understand because it was stated with tongue placed firmly in cheek.

Lake Willoughby

Willoughby Lake also boasts its own U.S.O. (Unidentified Swimming Object). Way back in 1854, a travel writer told how Willoughby's surface was sometimes violently agitated while the air stayed perfectly still. Some people blamed supernatural forces. Others, perhaps more scientifically minded, guessed the phenomenon was caused by mountain winds. Frankly, both explanations seem a little farfetched to me. I'd blame the monster, a hypothesis that perfectly blends supernatural and scientific speculation.

The sighting of what we might call the Willoughby Wisp that got the most publicity occurred on September 9, 1986. While sitting on a point in Westmore, Audrey Besse and her mother saw a long, dark creature with two or three humps swimming south in the middle of the lake. By the time Mrs. Besse got her camera, the monster had vanished.

Perhaps an ancestor of Mrs. Besse's monster was discussed a little more than a hundred years before in an issue of the St. Johnsbury *Caledonian*. The article said a 12-year-old boy, Stephen Edmonds, killed a giant snake in Willoughby Lake. Reportedly, the boy rushed the monster and cut it in half with a sickle. When the two pieces were measured, they were found to equal a length of 23 feet. Definitely not a grass snake.

My friend Bill Schubart, a Burlington businessman, used to summer on Lake Willoughby and recalls a similar story from the early '50s. Apparently, the son of a wealthy family was home on leave from the Navy. While sailing alone near Mt. Pisgah, his boat was hammered by a freak wind and capsized. The young sailor drowned, but his body never surfaced. The Navy dispatched a team of divers to recover the body. At 300 feet, the divers discovered a black hole that descended even farther. There the divers not only *saw* but reportedly *photographed* giant eels 6 to 8 feet long and as thick as telephone poles.

Can this be true? And if it is, where are the photographs?

Bill seems to recall they were kept by the town clerk in Westmore. If that was so, they have long since disappeared; today's assistant town clerk knows nothing about them. Mr. P.M. Daniels, who held the post in the early '50s, remembers the story, but doesn't recall the photographs. Could such eels exist? I asked him.

Maybe. Mr. Daniels himself has seen one 4 or 5 feet long!

Lake Memphremagog

Next to Champ, the best known of all Vermont's water monsters is said to live in Lake Memphremagog, a comparatively short distance from Lake Willoughby.

Oddly, Lakes Memphremagog and Willoughby are believed to be connected by underground channels as well as by the Barton and Willoughby Rivers. This suggests the two lakes could share the same family of monsters. At least the critters are described in pretty much the same way: 6 to 75 feet long, either smooth or scaly, with and without humps. This kind of precision might make it difficult to pick these mystery animals out of a line-up.

Sightings of Memphremagog's multiple-choice monster indicate it has been around for a long time. Legend says it frightened the Indians in pre-Colonial times, then went on to bamboozle the settlers. The monster was first reported in 1816, but until recently, fame eluded him.

Lake Memphremagog's first monster hunter was Uriah Jewett, a colorful local fisherman who lived on what is now called Jewett's Point. In the mid-1800s, he became obsessed with proving the existence of the beast. The townspeople laughed at him, calling the serpent "Uriah's Alligator." But Jewett was not to be dissuaded. He tried to catch it in traps baited with lambs' heads. Though consistently unsuccessful, he said the bait was always gone in the morning.

Jewett's theory was that the serpent had entered Memphremagog through a subterranean channel under Owl's Head (the deepest and most legend-laden part of the lake). But once in, the stupid animal couldn't find its way back to the Atlantic Ocean.

Over the years, monster sightings continued. During the last century, newspapers seemed to take great delight in featuring the beast, though like today, most sightings probably went unreported. I wonder how many witnesses kept their sightings secret, fearing the ridicule that plagued Uriah Jewett all his life?

Typical of nineteenth-century sightings, this is from the St. Johnsbury *Caledonian*, August 3, 1850: "About two weeks ago [the serpent] was seen distinctly by Uncle David Beebe while fishing off Magoon Point. . . . A sudden splash attracted his attention, and turning, he was astonished to behold the head and six feet of body of a huge monster, perfectly erect and graceful, apparently motionless. He was soon relieved, however, by the sudden and almost silent disappearance below the surface." The *Caledonian* concluded, "That a critter of the snake species does there exist, seems hardly to admit a doubt."

And the reports continued. Some are especially fascinating. For example, in 1935, the mayor of Newport, Frank D. Burns, disappeared and was presumed drowned. Divers looking for his body returned empty-handed. But they said they had seen giant "eels six to eight feet long and as thick as a man's thigh." (Note how similar this is to the Lake Willoughby story. In fact, it might be the same story! Given the reliability of memory, it's possible my friend Bill Schubart mixed up the two lakes. Or one lake borrowed the other's story. Such is the reliability of folklore.)

Along about the same time, Dr. Curtis Classen, a military surgeon from Brooklyn, New York, owned a house on the lake. On October 26, 1935, he was burning brush on the shore when he looked out at the water. There he saw an unfamiliar reptile that appeared very much like an alligator. As the creature crawled out of the water and onto the shore, Classen ran to the house to get his wife and her friend. All three reached the lake in time to see the animal vanish into the water, leaving nothing behind but some prints. The witnesses estimated the creature was 18 inches wide and about 10 feet long.

Dr. Classen's alligator sighting didn't vindicate Uriah Jewett. Instead, Classen was laughed at too. He did, however, consult a zoologist who contributed another layer to the mystery. The zoologist told him an alligator might be able to survive in the lake if it lived in the proximity of a warm spring. And there are warm springs that feed the lake at Bay View Point. Still the question remains: if it was an alligator, where did it come from?

The threat of laughter has always been a powerful tool of censorship. Surely it influenced a man from Irasburg who saw something swimming off the east shore of Newport Bay way back in 1939, but held his silence until quite recently.

In the 1940s, Hector Guyon had a cottage on the west shore of Memphremagog near Green Point. Every morning for a week, between 9:00 a.m. and midday, he'd watched a serpent lounging in the water about 300 feet from shore.

When he told his brother-in-law Noe Viens about it, Viens wanted to see for himself. He grabbed his rifle and the two men rowed out to where the serpent liked to sun himself. Viens saw it too. He described a gargantuan grass snake, 150 feet long and about a foot in diameter. It was coiled, its head rising a good 3 feet above the water. Viens fired a shot but missed. Then the creature ". . . made a great swell like a boat cutting through the water; an enormous wave."

More up-to-date encounters include Hank Dewey's great adventure. In the mid-'60s, Dewey, of Stanstead, Quebec, was fishing in his little boat along with two women friends. Suddenly a "big fish," or maybe a snake, surfaced near them. Whatever it was started to chase their boat. It pursued them until they had moored, leaving the women so shaken they vowed never to go on the lake again.

In 1972, a group of people on a yacht near Owl's Head saw the beast. And that same year, a scuba diver looking for underwater caves had a subsurface encounter.

Perhaps the most dramatic 1972 sighting occurred on a warm, clear summer night. Helen Hicks of West Main Street in Newport, then director of the Red Cross of Essex County, was relaxing with some friends on a boat. At around 10:00 p.m., she saw "a creature which had . . . a face somewhat like a horse, with two very red eyes and a body . . . 75 to 100 feet long. . . . The neck appeared to be very long; the back had . . . an appearance of scales, large ones. . . . A spotlight was put on it from the boat, and then it started to come for the boat. It rolled over . . . causing the boat to be very tippy. It shorted out the boat motor."

And in June or July of 1976, a local man was fishing when he saw "a seal with a long neck. . . . It was black and well above the water."

Multiple-Choice Monsters

BY NOW we have begun to see what is especially odd about Memphremagog's Mystery Monster. Unlike Champ, who, when sighted in the water, is consistently described as a "water horse," Memphremagog's USO is described in wildly different ways.

And this has been the case for a long time. The curious phenomenon was noted more than a half-century ago by an anonymous local poet whose verse was reproduced in William Bullock's *Beautiful Waters*, vol. 2:

"Eyes saw the monster, but none saw alike,
He was half serpent, half horse, some said,
While others formed him like a huge long pike
With thick, bright scales and round, not flattened head."

Descriptions of the monster are so diverse that several basic categories can be identified: 1. the long-necked seal; 2. the sea horse; 3. the long-snouted alligator, which, admittedly, is similar to the 4. "giant pike" sightings; 5. the "living log" and finally, 6. the snake or sea serpent with humps, of which the "giant eels" may be considered a subdivision.

It is consistently described as moving fast, leaving a large wake and exhibiting curiosity about its human observers. Some who see it go so far as to say the creature projects a certain gentleness in its big dark eyes. (Again, quite different from Ms. Hicks's ". . . horse, with two very red eyes," which sounds almost demonic.)

It's easy to see why, with this apparent propensity for shape-shifting, the monster can take on an air of the supernatural.

And if it's currently perceived as gentle, this has not always been the case. As far as I know, Memphremagog's monster is the only Vermont aquatic anomaly with a checkered past.

Even today, folks around the lake recall how the old-timers used to tell children not to get too close to the water—otherwise the sea serpent might gobble them up!

Bullock believed that the creature's fearsome nature was integral to pre-Colonial Indian beliefs. "It is said they were quite terrified, that they dared not swim the lake for fear of being devoured by the monster."

In the first volume of his *Beautiful Waters*, Bullock passes along Derby writer Norman Bingham's sea serpent legends, including the horrible murder of an Indian woman by her husband. The serpent drank her blood, feasted on her cadaver and grew phenomenally large. Then, having developed a taste for humans, began to patrol the lake looking for more of the newfound delicacy. Later, the monster, "dark and green . . . with lifted head and tusk and horn" and looking like "a furious horse" caught the murderer on the lake and devoured him, canoe and all. Then it returned to its cavernous home under Owl's Head.

Perhaps the monster or its more peaceful progeny have lost their taste for human flesh, but as we have seen, they *will* chase boats once in a while.

Memphre

In 1983, something happened that would change the status of Memphremagog's Monster and the course of its history. Barbara Malloy, a housewife from Newport, along with her two children and mother-in-law, saw a dark brown creature with a head like a horse swimming below Shattuck Hill.

Malloy wasn't about to keep such an experience a secret. It piqued her curiosity as well as her courage: in effect, she became determined to bring the monster to the surface. Together with Jacques Boisvert, a scuba diver and historian from Magog, Quebec, Malloy co-founded the International Dracontology Society of Lake Memphremagog. They coined the term "dracontology" to mean, essentially, the study of dragons; and they even christened the animal "Memphre," the only lake monster with a French name (though some might argue that it's an Indian name). In spite of its name, they awarded it dual citizenship, seeing Memphre as a symbol of free trade and lasting friendship between Canada and the United States.

Though Boisvert has never seen the creature, he doesn't doubt the witnesses who have. (However, he does recall a night dive during which, "I landed on a small black log, and when I touched it, the log moved away!")

Boisvert and Malloy discovered, investigated and recorded over 130 sightings documented by over 200 individuals, most of them people without cameras. Or sickles.

Malloy herself had an opportunity to photograph the beast in 1989, but the results were inconclusive. The society offers a reward of $1,000 for an indisputable photograph.

Because of the team's work, the cities of Magog and Newport proclaimed the beast a "protected species" in 1986. The Dracontologists do all they can to interest scientists in searching for and identifying their unknown aquatic neighbor, knowing full well that an organized search could be a big, expensive job: the lake is about 30 miles long, a mile wide and extremely deep in places. And to complicate things further, there's that legend about Memphremagog being connected to other lakes by a maze of underground rivers . . .

In 1992, the Dracontology Society logged eight sightings, one of which added a new detail to the description: Memphre was reported to be making a sound like a dolphin! This, like the on-land sighting reported in 1935, is very rare, perhaps unique.

Like all his arcane kin, Uriah's Alligator has clung to life and has slithered through the twentieth century. Now it's about to plunge into the twenty-first. I hope the International Dracontology Society can keep up with the creature, carrying on Uriah's work . . . and his obsession.

But it will be difficult. After all, when any one spot of the big lake is under observation, think of all the unobserved water. It is there that these creatures seem to make their home—just out of sight and just out of camera range.

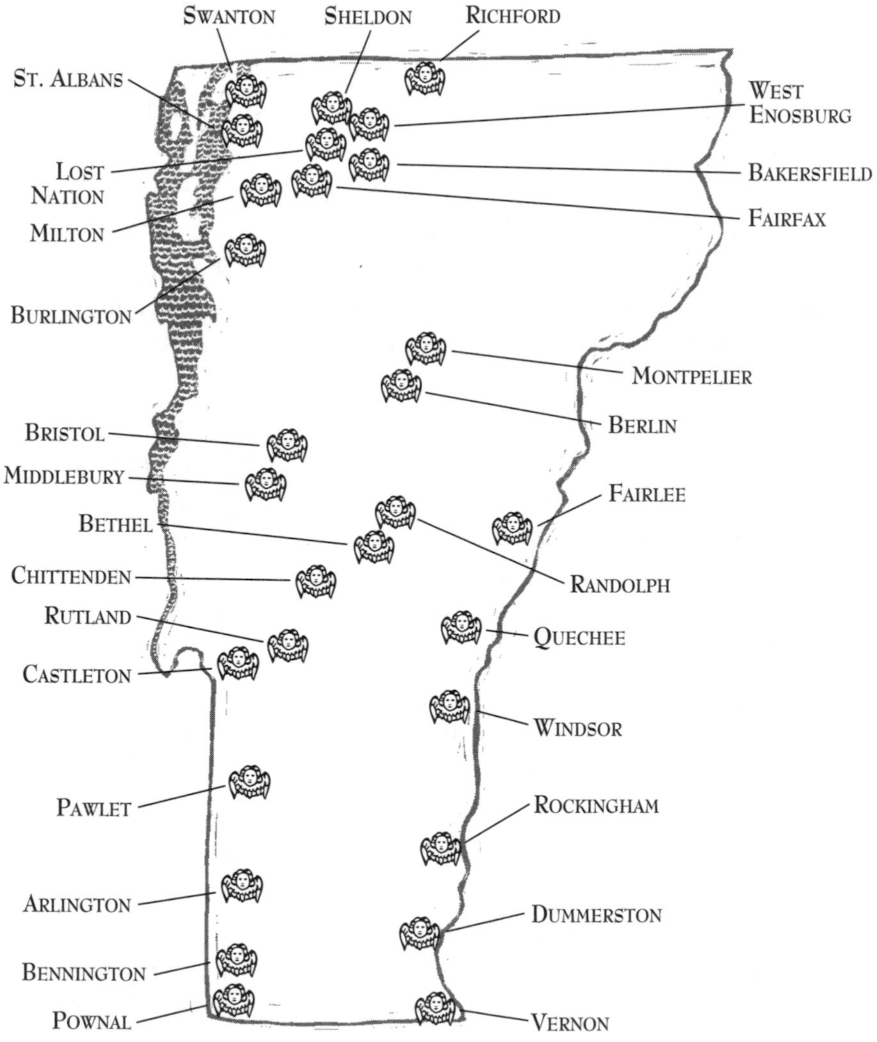

SWANTON
SHELDON
RICHFORD
ST. ALBANS
WEST ENOSBURG
LOST NATION
BAKERSFIELD
MILTON
FAIRFAX
BURLINGTON
MONTPELIER
BERLIN
BRISTOL
MIDDLEBURY
FAIRLEE
BETHEL
CHITTENDEN
RANDOLPH
RUTLAND
QUECHEE
CASTLETON
WINDSOR
PAWLET
ROCKINGHAM
ARLINGTON
DUMMERSTON
BENNINGTON
POWNAL
VERNON

Alien Skies

One cultural enigma that has plagued mankind for years has to do with weird things in the sky—things that can't be explained, can't be recognized, and probably shouldn't be there at all. I'm talking about Unidentified Flying Objects, UFOs.

Like ghosts and water monsters, UFOs are a worldwide phenomenon. It can be argued that there is nothing uniquely "Vermonty" about them—except maybe the one Don Pratt spotted in Bennington in September 1984. He said it looked like a "flying silo."

But silos aren't the only soaring shapes Vermonters have reported. They've seen things that look like saucers, cigars, cylinders, sickles, washtubs, swastikas, steam irons, boomerangs, triangles, fishing lures, even bathtubs. And the objects vary from about the size of a football to as big as a whole football field.

Mysterious flying shapes have been seen all over the state in every county, maybe in every town. They've been reported from as far south as Bennington all the way to the Canadian border—with particularly active "hotspots" along the Connecticut River and in the Northwestern corner of the state, especially Westford and Richford.

So what are people seeing? Extraterrestrial tourists? Flatlanders from far-off galaxies? Sunspots or swamp gas?

Possibly the explanations are disappointingly prosaic, like weird weather phenomena or experimental aircraft the government hasn't seen fit to tell us about.

Who knows? Only the witnesses. And many of them don't know for sure.

Lost Nation

Some claim the modern age of UFO sightings began in the 1940s, somehow provoked by atmospheric disturbances caused by the war and the first detonations of atomic weapons. The sightings carried over into the '50s when the various space programs began.

But Vermonters had seen odd aerial enigmas long before anyone thought about nuclear warfare or the space race.

For well over half a century, the so-called "Lost Nation" area—almost on the East Fairfield-Bakersfield line—has been home for farmers Doris and Lemond Bovat.

There, sightings of odd airborne objects were routine for both of them, especially Doris, who'd been aware of peculiar lights in the woods all her life. Even when she was a girl in the early part of this century, people talked about the small red, glowing balls that were often seen flying around in the bushes.

A modern sighting illustrates the kind of thing Doris had heard about. In 1975, Robert Nickson, a teacher at Syracuse University, was staying at his cabin in the same Lost Nation area. It was night. The cabin door was open. Suddenly, a basketball-sized light appeared outside, hovering about 8 feet off the ground. It was a red, glowing sphere that moved to within 15 feet of Nickson. "It made a sort of ticking noise every few minutes," he recalled.

Nickson invited the object to come in, but it took off instead. He must have scared it.

Doris herself recalls a number of encounters on her Lost Nation farm. One especially dramatic sighting occurred in the early '70s. "I was looking out the doorway and I saw this rounded pale orange disk about 400 or 500 feet up in the air, moving pretty fast, north to south. I ran out of the house to watch it. It looked like a pretty good-sized washtub."

Doris thought the object crashed into the woods of a mountaintop.

Before that, around 1958, Lemond Bovat had his own encounter. He claims to have seen something that looked like the full moon moving close to the ground. When it started moving rapidly toward him, he had to jump into a ditch to avoid being hit.

Perhaps the golden age of well-documented Vermont UFO sightings predates the 1940s. There is good evidence it began on July 2, 1907, on a street corner in Burlington. The following eyewitness testimony was weird enough to be included in Charles Fort's *The Book of the Damned*:

"I was standing on the corner of Church and College Streets, just in front of the Howard Bank, and facing east, engaged in conversation with [two other men] when, without the slightest indication, or warning, we were startled by what sounded like a most unusual and terrific explosion, evidently very nearby. Raising my eyes and looking eastward along College Street, I observed a torpedo-shaped body, some 300 feet away, stationary in appearance, and suspended in the air about 50 feet above the tops of the buildings. In size it was about 6 feet long by 8 inches in diameter, the shell, or covering, having a dark appearance, with here and there tongues of fire issuing from spots on the surface, resembling red-hot, unburnished copper. Although stationary when first noticed, this object soon began to move, rather slowly, and disappeared over Dolan Brothers' Store, southward. As it moved, the covering seemed rupturing in places, and through these the intensely red flames issued."

With a story of this kind, the first thing we want to check on is the credibility of the witnesses. In this case, their credentials are pretty impressive. The writer was Vermont Roman Catholic Bishop John S. Michaud. His companion was ex-Governor of the state of Vermont Urban Woodbury.

Though we may assume the report is accurate, we still don't know what they actually saw. One wonders what could have caused such an explosion in an era long before jet airplanes and sonic booms. What was in the skies in those days that could be described as torpedo-shaped, 6 feet long, apparently metallic and giving off flames? This all happened at the turn of the century, remember. Back then what could hover motionless in the air, then move slowly away?

Whatever Bishop Michaud and Governor Woodbury saw definitely wasn't a helicopter.

Today we might say the men saw a flying saucer.

The familiar term "flying saucer" is relatively new. It came into existence in 1947 when Kenneth Arnold, a civilian airplane pilot, saw nine disk-shaped objects flying in formation over Mount Rainier in Washington state. When a newspaperman picked up the story, he christened the disks "flying saucers."

After Arnold's sighting, the whole country went flying saucer crazy. There were sightings reported coast to coast in almost every state.

Mrs. Albert Steele of Rutland is credited with seeing Vermont's first flying saucer. It was 2:05 a.m. July 7, 1947, thirteen days after Arnold's sighting.

She observed the object from her bedroom window during a rainstorm. Mrs. Steele said its glow lit the sky so brightly that she thought it was morning.

She described it this way: "It was oval-shaped and there were jagged edges sticking out in all directions. The edges were different colors, but the center was like a brilliant white light." Mrs. Steele said the object was stationary in the sky over the Central Vermont Public Service Corporation.

Saucers Abound

SINCE THEN, flying saucers have been seen in Vermont skies nearly every year. In fact, one could almost take a flying saucer tour of the state by driving north along Route 7, then following the Canadian border to Newport and heading south beside the Connecticut river.

Moving north from Pownal, here are a few stops along the way:

Back in 1966, the rainy night of April 24 was filled with mystery for Robert Martin of Bennington. At about 2:15 a.m., Martin was in the Pownal Valley, driving home along Route 7. Just beyond the Warren Wire Company, "a big light suddenly came on about 200 yards away and at the height of the Bennington Monument above the ground." Martin said the object was "like someone was holding a big oil drum lit on fire. . . . It was like a torch with color changing." The object dimmed a little and gave off what Martin describes as a "jet tail." He said, "This jet tail was definitely contained as though coming from a tube of some sort." Then, from the bottom of the object, "red-hot coals" started to drop toward the ground, where they went out. Martin never stopped driving and eventually lost sight of the object. "If you don't think this didn't give me goose bumps you've got another think coming," he said. "I saw this thing, but I wish I hadn't. I hope I never see another one."

And it was in Bennington, early September 1984, that Don Pratt saw what he described as a "flying silo." Many other people saw Pratt's silo between 1978 and 1984, often in the vicinity of Battenkill Road, Orber Road or above the mountains near Manchester. Most described it as fat and round and about 60 feet long.

In Arlington, a schoolteacher driving on Battenkill Road saw the craft and thought it was going to land in a nearby cornfield. It didn't.

Other people saw it too. Amid six witnesses, one man aimed a rifle at it, hoping to see it more clearly through the scope. According to the witnesses, there was a bright flash and the flying silo disappeared. However, the man said he'd caught a glimpse of strange markings on the side.

September 19, 1984: Mrs. Hurley was driving her pickup along Orber Road near Bennington. She was hurrying to pick up a babysitter when she saw a bright light in the road in front of her. It's a jeep, she thought, and sounded her horn. The "jeep" got out of her way, all right. Mrs. Hurley reports it rose into the air and floated over the cab of her truck. As it passed above her, she felt a horrible burning sensation in her cheek. Frightened, she turned around and drove home, feeling dizzy and nauseated. When her husband saw that her skin was covered by little boils, he insisted that she visit their doctor at once. The doctor said she was suffering from prickly heat.

During the same month, the Williams family of Pawlet repeatedly spotted a UFO over the nearby mountains. It was a disk 40 feet long and 10 feet across. Mrs. Williams said it was "like the end of a football, only rounder."

Moving on to Rutland, the birthplace of Vermont's flying saucers, witnesses saw a cylinder-shaped craft "with a red beam of light" over the General Electric Research Center building. Oddly, a similar UFO had been spotted over the same building back in 1978. Some sort of intergalactic industrial espionage, perhaps?

On October 18, 1984, Pratt's Silo, or something similar to it, was spotted over Chittenden. A police officer said it seemed to be 150 feet in diameter. He also saw "a little craft come out of it."

In nearby Castleton, on March 30, 1966, Gladys Mattison and her son Edward saw a UFO behind their house. Edward saw it first while outside getting a pail of water. As he approached the brook, the saucer flew up into the air in front of him as if he had startled it. When he heard unusual sounds in the nearby bushes, he ran into the house. Mrs. Mattison saw the saucer hovering there. It was red on the bottom, white on top and about 15 feet across. And it made a whirring sound. She raced to the phone and called the state police. In the midst of her report, she heard something prowling outside. Whatever it was crossed the wooden bridge by her house and vanished into the woods.

Police investigated but found nothing.

Continuing north to Middlebury, near the Middlebury-Weybridge line, a teenager reported "a cigar shaped object with lighting at each end" hovering in the northeast corner of the night sky during February 1980. He said he "had been watching the thing for more than an hour" before he phoned police to see if anyone else had noticed it. After a while, the object dropped out of sight below the tree line. Police investigators found nothing. Nine days before, in Burlington, traffic controllers at the Burlington International Airport—and local police—said they saw a UFO. Controller Donald Kernan said the UFO was a bright light that "did a kind of dance." Can there be a more credible witness than an air-traffic controller? Maybe a bishop and an ex-governor.

A "mass sighting" occurred in Burlington on March 13, 1965, when twenty-five people saw a UFO over the south end of the city. Tom Provost of Foster Street saw it approaching from Pine Street, moving toward Lake Champlain. It was yellow on top, blue on the bottom and had "a glow all over it." It would move rapidly, then stop. And when it was stationary, rays of red light shone down from the bottom. Provost and three friends chased it and split up to search. Alone on a path by the lake, Provost heard an odd noise above him. When he looked up, he saw the UFO. It moved above the lake where it dropped some red rays, then slipped behind the tree line and eventually vanished over New York state.

An alleged landing took place in Bristol on July 14, 1967. Mrs. Marjorie Pacquette spotted the UFO at 10:00 p.m. She insists she knew it was not the moon, a jet or a helicopter. As the object came closer, she and some friends decided to follow it in a car. They chased it to a field just off Plank Road, where they are certain they saw it land.

"We could see green lights in the fields and it had two sets of lights. It appeared to be 500 feet from us in John Kilburn's pasture."

Mrs. Veronica Mayer said when she saw the object drop into the field it appeared to have some sort of landing gear attached. After the UFO took off, Mrs. Pacquette walked around looking for evidence, but found none.

Moving further north, and jumping ahead in time to October 9,

1973 at 10:15 p.m., Mrs. John Bushey of St. Albans and Sandra Chagnon were driving on Route 89 near Milton when a brilliant ball of silver- yellow light zoomed by, just missing the front of their car. "It came upon us so suddenly we didn't have time to do anything," Mrs. Bushey said. "We were frightened."

The oval-shaped object was only about a car length ahead of them. Although they described it as glowing, it did not give off fire or sparks.

Up in the northwest corner of the state, the Franklin County area has been a hotbed of UFO activity for years.

On April 20, 1966, St. Albans policemen Arthur Brouillette and Wallace Guyette witnessed two brilliant objects hovering over the city. They were responding to a UFO call from City Attorney John Webster, a confirmed skeptic. Captain Terrance Flanagan also saw the aerial display. One object was reddish orange, the other white. The objects moved out over the lake and eventually vanished.

Twenty years later, in 1986, dozens of Franklin County residents reported seeing a delta-shaped flying object with a bright white light in front and small red, white and green lights underneath. The craft apparently hovered and soared. Although physical descriptions were similar, reports differed on the sound it made. Some people said it was silent; others reported a giant whoosh.

In any event, sightings were so common that the object became known as The Franklin County UFO.

In the area between Bakersfield and St. Albans, a barber named Joe Cofelice and his son Jimmy were driving west along Town Road 20 at 7:50 p.m. on November 10, 1981. "We saw two lights on the left that seemed to be pacing us. They looked like large stars, but they were coming closer, then suddenly shot up straight in the air."

The Cofelices rounded a bend and saw the lights again, 200 yards away, 200 feet up, blinking on and off. "They lit up the whole road like daylight." Joe got out of the car and walked toward them. The lights took off, but when they crossed the moon he got a look at them. "They had square wings on each side and round backs. In front there was a half circle of seven lights."

Two nights later, Joe and his fiancee, Laurie, returned to the spot with binoculars and a camera. He said, "Lo and behold, at exactly 7:50 again, the lights came at us from the west."

When they were 500 yards away Laurie took a photograph. The developed picture was examined by the Center for UFO Studies in Evanston, Illinois, but the photo showed only a round light against a black background, which couldn't be identified.

In Swanton during October 1985, Slim Bovatt was watching television one night when he saw a light outside his picture window. "It was a very bright light," he said, "bright as an electrical welder's light." Bovatt said he'd seen falling stars and shooting stars, but never anything like that. Stranger still, he said whatever it was appeared to drop right into Lake Champlain! In St. Albans at about the same time, a woman driving down Lake Street corroborated that whatever it was seemed to disappear into the lake. "It was a really bright glow," she said, and speculated that it might have been a meteorite.

In February of 1982, a Bakersfield woman named Aubre Brogden had a terrifying experience with a UFO. She was driving home from St. Albans on a clear night, under a full moon. At about 9:00 p.m., she saw a large white light low in the sky, moving slowly. "At first I thought it was a plane about to land, so I flashed my car headlights to warn it off the road. And then it started coming towards me!"

As it got closer, Ms. Brogden perceived it as triangular. No doubt it's just a balloon or a hang-glider, she thought.

When she got home, she found it was waiting for her in her backyard. "It was just hovering there, about 25 feet away from me.

"I got out of the car, picked up my two bags of groceries and started toward the house. Then I stopped for a moment to look at the thing and began to feel very frightened. It was obviously watching me."

Brogden dropped her groceries and ran for the house. "The thing was then moving right over my head, making absolutely no sound. Now I could see that it wasn't just one light, it had many lights all across the bottom. And it was much bigger than I'd thought, maybe as big as a football field."

After the object vanished from sight, the frightened Aubre called a neighbor to come and spend the night. Neither woman went outside to get the groceries.

A month later, twelve members of a PTA group spotted something in the same area. "We were en route to Fairfield for a meeting," Jan Marcotte said. "I saw four blinking red lights at different elevations. We stopped our car, but the others kept going. We got out to look but didn't hear any sound. Then suddenly the lights just disappeared."

In June of 1986, witnesses in Fairfax described "two cylinders that coupled together into a massive triangular craft."

Bill Moore and his twin sons saw a delta-shaped something in East Enosburg. And in West Enosburg, a woman claimed the craft hovered over her home and shone a bright light into her picture window. Up at the Canadian border, in Richford, five guys working the second shift at the Blue Seal Feed Plant saw The Franklin County UFO—or something very like it.

Reversing our direction at the border and heading south again, let's pause in Central Vermont to check out a sighting that occurred right on the Interstate in August 1987. A popular Vermont folksinger and her companion were driving on I-89 near Berlin. At about 1:00 a.m., they saw something strange above the trees. Though the object was dark, they could see it was a huge inverted pyramid with lights on each of its corners.

She admitted she had been feeling sleepy before she saw the thing. When I asked her if it could possibly have been a dream or hallucination she said "No." Both people in the car had seen it, and the impact of the surreal and startling vision "got our adrenalin going." The object paced their car for a while, then took off at a fantastic speed and vanished.

The singer told me she really couldn't estimate its speed, distance from the car, or its elevation, but she remembers being impressed by its apparent size, "as big as a three-story building."

A Classic Encounter

NOW LET'S TAKE A LOOK at one of Vermont's "classic" UFO episodes. By classic I mean an encounter that is more than routinely dramatic, gets wide media exposure, and in which the witnesses have exceptional credibility.

January 4, 1965. Route 12, someplace between Bethel and Randolph. Quarter after five in the afternoon. It was dark but the weather was clear. Stars were perfectly visible; there was no moon.

The principal witness was Dr. Richard Woodruff, Vermont's chief medical examiner, respected scientist and faculty member at UVM.

It seems especially significant to me that Dr. Woodruff was returning to Burlington after providing testimony in a case before a grand jury in Brattleboro—he was an expert witness.

His companion, a high-ranking state policeman, had also testified.

By virtue of their professions, both men were accustomed to making accurate observations and giving precise statements.

And both men agree about what happened.

Suddenly, above some treetops to their left, an object appeared. It was sharply defined, glowing orange-red, and a little less bright than an automobile headlight. The object crossed the highway in front of their car at a terrific speed.

"My God, did you see that?" the policeman asked.

Just as he spoke, a second object came into view, following the first. Then a third object did the same thing. They were identical and appeared at precise intervals, all holding the same flight path and altitude. They climbed slightly, moving west to east, then zipped into the distance and faded away.

Viewed through the automobile windshield, the objects appeared to be solid. They looked round, though the men couldn't determine the exact shape because of the great velocity: faster than a jet—maybe as much as 2,000 miles per hour.

Size was tough to estimate, too, but the men agreed they looked about as big as a football held at arm's length. Their best guess was that the objects were a half mile to one mile away.

The men figured the whole sighting lasted only about thirty seconds. Neither heard any sounds from the glowing lights.

Dr. Woodruff reported the sighting to the *Burlington Free Press* and to Edward Knapp, then head of the state Aeronautics Board. Many New England papers quickly picked up the story. Later it was written up in a number of journals and books about UFOs.

Dr. Woodruff admitted that he had been reluctant to report the incident and to notify the press. "I know everything I saw will be open to misinterpretation," he said. "But remember, two of us saw the same thing at the same time. I was not seeing things . . . I am not . . . overly imaginative and neither is the trooper."

Although all the courts in Vermont sought Dr. Woodruff's expert testimony, Air Force representatives—none of whom had seen the objects or visited the site—dismissed the whole episode with great authority. The Pentagon, through their public information officer, a Major Jacks, said, "The UFOs were only meteors."

"I am amazed that the Major could not come up with a better solution . . ." Dr. Woodruff responded. "If I had thought that there was a possibility that the three objects we saw were meteors, I never would have mentioned the matter. . . . While I make no speculation as to what the objects . . . might be, I do feel most definitely that they were not meteors."

And of course he was right. Meteors come down haphazardly, not in formation. And they fall much faster than 2,000 miles per hour. Then they all do one of two things: they either burn up in the atmosphere or they hit the earth. It would be impossible for three identical meteors to descend together, slow down, level off in precise line formation, then soar off again into the sky.

The same "meteors" were seen by four people in the car following Dr. Woodruff's. And Hugh E. Wheatley, Chairman of the Randolph Board of Selectmen, saw the same thing.

Moving East

AT THIS POINT, we'll direct our Odyssey of the Orbs back along the eastern side of the state, following the Connecticut River south. In Fairlee, two witnesses reported an exceedingly odd sight. They said they saw "two 60-foot-long cylinders in the sky connecting together," with two more nearby. As the combined craft started rising, the other two cylinders connected with it, forming a massive metal contraption. "Six to nine disks the size of Volkswagens entered" the structure. Then the entire complex vanished into the sky.

Quechee. November 16, 1973. 8:30 p.m. Patrolman Stephen Broughall of the Hartford Police Department responded to a call from four Quechee teenagers, Kevin and Kim Potter, and Sharon and Patrick Rice. Broughall joined them and watched the silent object for seventeen minutes. He said it was yellow and orange and appeared to be 300 feet off the ground, moving behind the Congregational Church. It suddenly turned bright white and sped off into the sky. Officer Broughall had trouble making his radio work during the sighting. A ten-year veteran of the force, Broughall admitted he had never seen anything like it.

In Windsor, the birthplace of Vermont, back in April of 1981, two Vermont Public Radio employees—Linda Kingsbury and Lucy Slothower—were coming out of a grocery store at about 7:30 one Wednesday night when they saw a star that seemed to be moving. More precisely, it seemed to be moving right at them! The women say the object flew directly over their heads.

Ms. Slothower, then assistant development director of VPR, said, "It was an enormous craft, shaped like a triangle with a grid system in between, and lights outlining the structure."

She said, "The object moved *slowly*. . . . [As it] approached I could hear what sounded like an engine, a big heavy hum."

Ms. Slothower came to her own conclusion about what she saw and was quite emphatic about saying so, "There was no way it could be an airplane. It was a spacecraft. . . ."

The craft was so quiet and "subtle" that Ms. Slothower doubts it would have been seen "by anyone driving down the road." However, it turns out many witnesses saw a similar object in the same area.

Another of Vermont's classic sightings occurred in Rockingham during December of 1966. This one made the news all around the world. It all started with two 14-year-old boys and a covered bridge.

Danny Gay and Ricky Sharp were on their way to photograph the Gageville covered bridge when they spotted a doughnut-shaped UFO hovering nearby. The object was noiseless, black and white, and had a "shiny coil on its dome." It appeared to be 25 feet in diameter. Ricky had the presence of mind to snap six pictures before the object zoomed straight up and out of sight. The boys told their parents and friends, but no one believed them. However, Tony Redington of the Bellows Falls *Times Reporter* listened to their story and agreed to develop the film. When he saw the photos, he immediately notified the National Investigation Committee on Aerial Phenomena whose representative, Walter Hicken of Keene, New Hampshire, said the photos were the best he'd ever seen. The photographs were reproduced in publications including *Look* and *Time*. The negatives were sent to Washington and may still be on file there.

And the UFOs continue to fly.

The real Vermont hotspot seems to be Bakersfield and the surrounding towns. This Franklin County area, as we have seen, has long been known as an active area.

Journalist Stefan Hard of the Enosburg Falls *County Courier* has been tracking a number of dramatic encounters.

For example, on Saturday, November 27, 1993 three teenagers, Errin Hartigan, Justine Macris and Luke Hardy, all seniors at Enosburg Falls High School, were driving along Route 36 near the Bakersfield-Fairfield town line. At about 10:30 at night they saw an "eggplant-shaped" object hovering overhead. "It was a white light. At first I thought it was a streetlight," Ms. Hartigan said, "But then I realized it was too high."

Luke Hardy thought it was a planet, "but it was too big, and it was in front of the clouds."

Justine Macris said, "It was almost like headlights in brightness."

All three agreed the shape of the object was an imperfect oval with an aura of brightness around it. The teenagers were convinced it was hovering, not moving, and that it wasn't a plane or helicopter. The young women became frightened when they thought the object might be watching them.

The trio observed the UFO for up to three minutes. During that time, they traveled at 25 miles per hour from the bridge just east of East Fairfield village along Route 36 to where John Howrigan's barn used to be, a distance of about a quarter mile.

When Luke Hardy stuck his head through the open sunroof to get a better look, the object vanished. Ms. Macris said, "It just disappeared. It didn't move away, it just disappeared.

Later, when they told their classmates about the sighting, they learned other students had seen other aerial phenomena.

And something very different moved across the night skies over Franklin County on Sunday, January 9, 1994.

Tom and Trudy Bryce, of Bridge Street in Sheldon, were lying in bed watching television at about 9:15 p.m. when Tom saw lights outside the window.

"My God, that's really weird," he said.

Trudy thought he was seeing headlights so she told him, "It's just a car."

"But Trudy," Tom said, "it can't be a car; there's no road there!"

They turned down the television and opened the window. Although they could hear nothing, the moving light was quite obvious as it progressed slowly at an altitude of about 100 feet. They examined it more closely with their binoculars. It appeared to be a square or rectangular in shape, Trudy said, but it "looked transparent, almost like you could see in, like one big window."

She described the object as having two bright white lights on one side with a fainter line of white lights around the perimeter.

Finally it disappeared from view, heading west in the direction of St Albans.

That same night, at about the same time, Leonard Weed was walking home from a friend's house. Pausing near Duffy Hill Road, he looked toward the village of Enosburg Falls and saw bright lights above the Community Health Center on Route 105.

He watched the UFO hovering there for three or four minutes as he continued home. He called to his wife, Leah, and together they watched the mysterious lights heading west.

"It appeared to be square, actually two squares joined together," Mrs. Weed said. She, too, perceived the structure as being almost transparent, "like a window lighted up with lights around each side. The two square sections remained joined together as they moved."

Although Leonard wasn't frightened by the sight, it made Leah "a little jittery."

"I think they're from another planet," she said. "They're not any experimental craft. . . . I think they're observing us, but I don't know what they're up to in Vermont on a 28 below zero night."

Good question.

At this point, we have completed our UFO tour of Vermont. We have come full circle, and in all fairness, we don't know any more now than when we started.

What do all these sightings have in common? Maybe just one thing: to this day there is no definitive explanation.

Cow Kill

And speaking of events without explanations, let's stop in Dummerston to investigate another of Vermont's Unsolved Mysteries. Does it have anything to do with Flying Silos? Judge for yourself . . .

As we have seen, 1984 was a big year for UFOs.

During the wet and foggy nights of February 16 and 17, something mysterious occurred in an innocent-looking Dummerston barn. It was part of Honeymoon Valley Farm, owned by Robert Ranney and his wife, Judy. This picturesque spot between Route 5 and the

Connecticut River was hardly the sort of place to be visited by anything . . . unnatural.

Yet Ranney discovered a tragedy unlike anything he'd ever seen before. It happened about three o'clock in the morning. "That's when I go out after the milking cows," Mr. Ranney told a reporter from the *Brattleboro Reformer.* He said, ". . . I have to go by the barn where the heifers are kept. I saw one heifer that looked like she might need help. And I looked in the barn. . . ."

What he saw was a gruesome sight that would be with him for the rest of his life. Twenty-three of his twenty-nine heifers were dead. According to Robert Ellis Cahill's account in *New England's Visitors From Outer Space*, the heifers were lying in a perfect circle with feed still in their mouths. The surviving six cows were perfectly all right.

The first thing Ranney did was call a veterinarian who performed an autopsy and determined that the animals had been electrocuted. He also assured Ranney that the animals had died instantly. What made the incident more mysterious was that there were no signs of a struggle or evidence that the young dairy cows had tried to escape. Whatever happened must have happened very fast.

Considering the value of the livestock—worth over a thousand dollars each—an insurance investigator inspected the scene. He agreed that all twenty-three cows had died instantly, probably by electrocution. And he added that it would be impossible for anyone to do such a thing intentionally. With that conclusion, foul play was ruled out, giving the incident an added layer of mystery.

More investigators checked the scene, including electricians, but no one could discover a reason for the eerie electrical deaths.

Ranney voiced a theory of his own, "What it looked like was lightning. . . . I've seen plenty of cows hit by lightning out in the field, and that's what these cows looked like."

Although lightning may seem the likely culprit, author Robert Cahill pointed out that "the barn doors were closed, there were no holes or scorch marks on the barn roof, and lightning surely would have torched the hay. Also, none of the dead cows had split hoofs, a sure sign that cows have been electrocuted by lightning."

Later, the most bizarre theory was put forth when another investigator showed up at Ranney's barn—an ex-policeman named William Chapleau of Rutland. Chapleau, profiled at length in the *Rutland Herald* in 1985, worked for a private organization called MUFON, an acronym for Mutual UFO Network.

Chapleau went over the scene with a Geiger-counter and found high radiation in the center of the barn and in the cornfield where the cows were buried. Noting the proximity of the farm to the Vermont Yankee Nuclear Power Plant in Vernon, Chapleau wondered if the animals might have been killed by some kind of freak radioactive release. He soon learned, however, that Yankee had been shut down at the time.

Then—having eliminated those possibilities—Chapleau speculated the animals may have been killed by a UFO.

On the night the cows died, four people had contacted him about a "torpedo-shaped" UFO over the Vernon Nuclear Plant. Also, a ball of light had been seen that same night in nearby Hinsdale, New Hampshire.

According to Cahill, no other explanation for the strange death of the animals has emerged.

Natural or unnatural causes? Who can say? If there is a connection between the cows, the UFO and the Nuclear Plant, the evidence seems entirely circumstantial.

Perhaps as we review all our UFO stories, certain minor patterns of questionable significance begin to emerge:

1. Individual UFOs are frequently seen to merge and thereby form more complex objects. In some cases, smaller objects seem to enter or leave bigger objects. What are we to make of this?

2. Often UFOs seem to be spotted in the proximity of scientific buildings or buildings related to power supplies: the Central Vermont Public Service Corporation, the General Electric Research Center and the Vermont Yankee Nuclear Power Plant. Some people around Manchester believe the UFO activity there is somehow related to abandoned copper mines in the area.

3. Sometimes an object seems to be watching the witness while the witness watches the object, such as in the Aubre Brogden episode,

the red orb encountered by Robert Nickson, and the woman from West Enosburg who claimed a craft shone a bright light through her picture window. And what about the witnesses who feel they are being "paced" by the flying object? Were Joe Cofelice of Bakersfield and the folksinger on Interstate 89 being watched?

4. Potentially more frightening are the cases when witnesses seem to be not only watched but also approached, even rushed, by the object as in the Brogden case, the sphere that drove Lemond Bovat into a ditch, and the adventure of the two VPR employees.

More disturbing still, do the mysterious objects sometimes become aggressive? Is it safe to say that a UFO somehow attacked Mrs. Hurley in her pickup when she felt "a horrible burning sensation" that left her dizzy, nauseated and covered with tiny boils?

And what about the cows at the Dummerston barn?

Patterns seem to exist, but they make no sense at all.

What Next?

OF COURSE, all these episodes are dependent on a witness's perceptions. And perceptions can be wrong. With that in mind, what about the UFO-related cases that get more and more "out of this world"? I'm talking about human-alien interaction, the so-called Close Encounters of the Third and Fourth Kind. Have such contacts occurred in the Green Mountain State? Well, maybe.

There's a case in western Vermont involving a farmer and his wife who suspected a bunch of kids were up to some mischief on their land. They crossed a cornfield to investigate. There—according to MUFON investigator William Chapleau—they came across a landed spaceship. A woman stood in the doorway of the ship signaling for the couple to come on board. Instead, they ran home, then tried to find someone to confirm what they had seen. When they returned to the field, the ship was gone.

In the past few years, these "encounters" have escalated to a new stage of weird. In the wake of such books and movies as *Communion* and

Intruders, there has been a lot of discussion about human beings who are abducted by aliens with mysterious, perhaps unfathomable motivations.

I talked to a woman, a former circus performer now living in northern Vermont, who says she has been abducted repeatedly over the course of her life. And I met three artists from southern Vermont who have been abducted together and individually. I also spoke with an abductee from central Vermont, a man with a background in politics and law enforcement.

Because of the horrifying nature of their abduction experiences, people hesitate to reveal their names and certain of the bizarre procedures they endured. In general, most of the people I talked to are ordinary in the positive sense. The only thing eccentric about them is that they claim to have been visited by tiny, frail and powerful creatures. Often these periodic visits began in childhood and continued for a lifetime.

Serious researchers like Dr. David M. Jacobs of Temple University and Dr. John Mack of Harvard have determined the abduction scenarios are highly structured. The abductee is somehow frozen, then transported by short, gray, insectlike beings who show little or no emotion. The victims are brought into "examining rooms" where they are treated in the cold, clinical manner typical of Nazi doctors. The creatures apparently communicate with each other, and with their victims, telepathically. They show no interest in the abductee as an individual. Their only concern seems to be human sexuality and any factor relating to childbearing.

After the diminutive creatures conduct the physical exam, taller beings stare deeply into the abductee's eyes. By so doing they can somehow extract information or create pictures in the victim's mind. Sometimes the process can produce an orgasm, which might include hallucinating intercourse. Sometimes pregnancies seem to result. Many female abductees recall being presented with so-called "wise babies," odd-looking hybrid infants and small children whom they assume to be their own.

As "far out" as these stories are, a growing number of scientists and psychologists are taking them seriously.

Some who have explored human-alien contact reports note how they resemble existing mythologies. Arguably, the most notable among these explorers is Dr. Jacques Vallee, a scientist turned UFO investigator. In his ground-breaking works, starting with *Passport to Magonia*, he has pointed out the similarities between these odd interspecies interactions and traditional fairy lore. In the latter case, humans were frequently "abducted" and carted off to fairy mounds where weird things were done to them.

Though generally considered more an Old World phenomenon, fairy encounters have happened here in Vermont. Consider the events discussed by Sir Arthur Conan Doyle and Rudyard Kipling in 1894 in Brattleboro:

Apparently, a Reverend Baring-Gould was traveling by carriage to Montpelier. When almost there, he was besieged by "legions of dwarfs about two feet high running along beside the horses. Some sat laughing on the pole, some were scrambling up the harness to get on the backs of the horses."

Was this an attempted abduction?

Were the "dwarfs" fairies or a nineteenth-century perception of diminutive UFO occupants?

Did Reverend Baring-Gould's encounter include a "missing time" experience?

All good questions without good answers. Of course, quaint scenarios such as this have been rendered obsolete by twentieth-century technology. Still, the similarities are striking. The impression of a tiny fairy standing under a toadstool is not far different from that of a little man standing under a saucer.

The era in which we live influences the way we see things. Before 1894, people just weren't thinking about extraterrestrials and interdimensional beings—not as we think of them today. If UFO contact is on a continuum with fairy lore, we may be witnessing an old myth all dressed up in late-twentieth-century fashions. Or perhaps we're witnessing a whole new type of folklore being born.

But whatever the source of the new myth, whether these human-alien confrontations are subjective or objective reality, the result is the same: people report that strange things happen to them.

With that in mind, let's take a look at a bizarre event that happened in northwestern Vermont, and not so very long ago . . .

Most people agree the age of well-documented, thoroughly researched UFO abductions began in the White Mountains of New Hampshire when Betty and Barney Hill were taken back in 1961. Walter N. Webb, assistant to the head of the Hayden Planetarium in Boston, investigated the Hill case. Later, he initiated a five-year study of a remarkably similar kidnapping that took place in 1968 in Vermont.

North of Burlington, at a private girls' camp on Lake Champlain, two employees—a young man and a young woman—were relaxing at water's edge. Almost at the same time, they noticed a bright object in the southwestern sky. It appeared starlike, but it was too bright to be a star.

And it seemed to be moving.

Suddenly, the bright object picked up speed, moving downward. As it descended, three small glowing circles separated from it.

Witness #1 (a male who chooses to remain anonymous) says the three objects performed a sort of aerial ballet. Then one of them broke away and sped across the lake. It dipped, entered the water and remained submerged for a few seconds. When it emerged, it raced toward the dock and the two witnesses.

The male witness saw a transparent dome on top of the UFO. Through it, two entities were visible inside. Almost immediately—or so it seemed—they saw the domed disk speed away and vanish.

Both witnesses claim they didn't discuss the encounter after the fact. More puzzling, the woman claims she didn't even remember it.

When the camp closed two weeks later, both teenagers left for home.

But the story doesn't end there.

Continually troubled by the incident, the young man eventually sought psychological help, but results were slow in coming. After nearly ten years of discomfort, he finally approached the Center for UFO Studies in Evanston, Illinois. The center referred him to Walter Webb in Boston.

Reputedly a cautious and thorough investigator, Webb arranged

a meeting with the witness. And it was that 1978 meeting that launched Webb's five-year investigation.

Right away, he tracked down the second witness who was now married and living in the Southeast. She claimed to recall the bizarre aerial ballet over Lake Champlain. She also recalled how one object soared across the lake toward them. But that's about all she remembered.

By carefully questioning both witnesses, Webb learned there was a period of time unaccounted for. Something had happened during that "missing time" and neither witness could recall what.

Meanwhile, independent of the witnesses, Webb was doing a little checking on his own. He says, "Extensive background character checks revealed [the witnesses] to be honest, credible persons who did not perpetrate a hoax or suffer some sort of fantasy, either individually or collectively." (He was also able to locate corroborating witnesses who saw the UFO soaring *away* from the Lake Champlain camp.)

Months later, Webb supervised a face-to-face reunion of the two principal witnesses. He was careful to see that they did not exchange information about the "encounter" before they met.

After this brief meeting, Webb referred the witnesses to separate hypnotists. In independent sessions, the hypnotists tried to facilitate more complete recall.

The man remembered flying through space, then actually entering the UFO. Inside the craft, he discovered he was unable to move. Looking around, he saw his companion stretched out on a table.

Then suddenly he found himself standing before the craft's occupants. He said the entities were five to five and a half feet tall. They had large, long heads. Their arms and legs were strangely thin. Their hands were odd too; they had only three fingers. The little creatures wore tight-fitting green-colored clothing.

After reviewing the separate accounts of the experience, Webb found both the major and minor details matched to a startling degree. He said, "Perhaps the most striking convergence of detail was an instrument panel viewed by each abductee on the wall beyond their examination tables. This device was depicted in enough detail to furnish rather convincing evidence, in my opinion, of a shared abduction experience."

In time, I suspect we'll come to some fair-minded conclusions about the inspiration and meaning of these not-so-rare abduction experiences. But as of now, it's difficult to predict whether the solution will come from a psychiatrist, a physicist, a folklorist or a theologian.

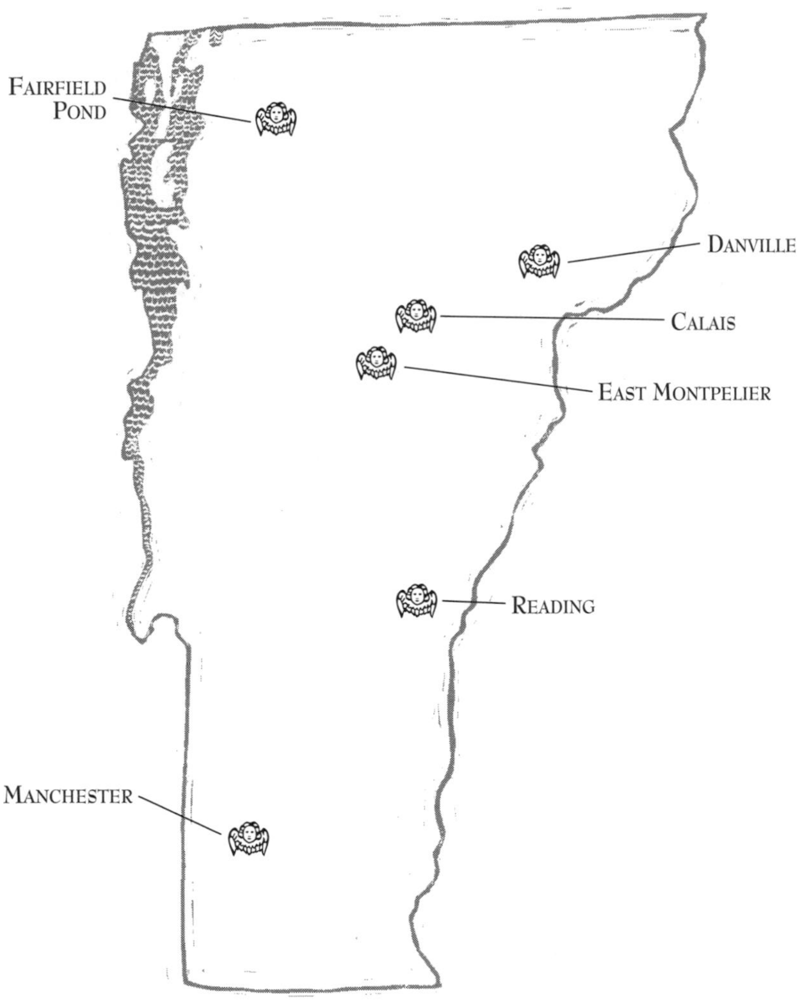

FAIRFIELD POND

DANVILLE

CALAIS

EAST MONTPELIER

READING

MANCHESTER

Perchance To Dream

Dreams have always played an important role in the folklore of the supernatural. Even today, many years after Freud articulated his theories about the subconscious mind, the *true* source and purpose of dreaming remains a mystery.

No one would argue that the dreamer enters an altered state. There, new worlds open up and strange things occur. We may visit remote lands, acquire special knowledge, gain awesome power. Or we may experience profound helplessness, grandiosity, visions, even premonitions. We could chat with deceased friends or be reunited with long-dead relatives who may sometimes seem strangely transfigured.

Generally, dream scenarios and dialogues are events the dreamer cannot control. It is easy, then, to believe that the source of the dream is separate from the dreamer.

And so dreams remain mystical, seemingly supernatural experiences. Some of us readily leap to the conclusion that dreams must be a psychic hotline for receiving instructions, warnings, reminders and important answers.

The following stories involve Vermonters who experienced particularly lucid dreams—dreams that altered the course of their lives. Conceivably, each story can conclude with the implicit, if melodramatic, last line:

It was all a dream. Or was it?

Boorn Again

THIS BIZARRE VERMONT MYSTERY has been written up in everything from history books to legal texts. For nearly 200 years, the events have fascinated readers, writers and criminologists. But elements of the gothic, the grotesque and the supernatural have fixed this tale permanently in the folk memory of our state.

The story began in the early 1800s in Manchester when Sally, the daughter of a hardworking farmer named Barney Boorn, married Russell Colvin. Trouble was, no one could figure out why.

Colvin was considered feeble-minded, lazy, maybe even "tetched"—given to strange habits like playing with toys and wandering off for days, even months at a time.

Because the couple lived with Sally's parents, Colvin hardly had to work for his keep. Colvin's "free ride" angered Sally's brothers, Jesse and Stephen. Not only did they have to work for what they had, but they were in danger of losing their inheritance to the shiftless Colvin.

"One of these days," Stephen Boorn once said, "I'll kick Russell to hell if I burn my legs off doing it."

Tension and family fighting continued until May of 1812 when Colvin—apparently up to his old tricks again—wandered off and didn't return. Some said he wanted to avoid the War of 1812. Others said he simply got sick of his wife's cooking. Everyone had a theory, but no one thought his disappearance was unusual.

The only real question was, Where'd he go?

Stephen added to the mystery when he told Sally, "Your stupid husband has gone where potatoes don't freeze."

Seven years passed, and Colvin didn't return. No one seemed especially sorry to be rid of him.

Then, in April of 1819, Amos Boorn, Sally's uncle, had a supernatural dream. The spontaneous message from the grave seemed especially urgent—so much so that the dream repeated three times.

In it, Colvin's ghost appeared and stood beside Amos's bed. The ghost said that he had been murdered and had come back to show Amos where his remains were buried. Uncle Amos's dream-self willingly followed the specter to the grave site.

Since Amos Boorn was "a man of unimpeachable integrity," a search was launched.

Oddly, remains *were* discovered in a place potatoes wouldn't freeze—an abandoned potato cellar in the field where Colvin had last been seen. Searchers found a button and a jackknife thought to be Colvin's. And a toenail and some bones, thought to be human.

Jesse and Stephen Boorn, loudly protesting their innocence, were arrested for the murder of Russell Colvin. Under the pressure of interrogation, Jesse confessed. He said that Stephen had killed Colvin. Stephen confessed, too, saying he'd quarreled with Colvin and hit him in the head—and that blow killed him. He further admitted that, yes, he'd hidden Colvin's body in the potato cellar. Then, fearing it might be discovered, he dug it up and threw it in the river.

An inconsequential dollop of doubt was cast on the confession when the unearthed bones were judged to be those of an animal. Still, the town went ahead with a murder trial based on the button, the knife, the toenail and the brothers' confessions. Even Russell Colvin's son, Lewis, testified that he'd seen Stephen fighting with his father. And that was on the last day Colvin had been seen alive, seven years before.

On the strength of this convergence of circumstance, the brothers were convicted and sentenced to be hanged. In appeal, Jesse's sentence was reduced to life in prison, but Stephen's death sentence was upheld. He, after all, had struck the killing blow.

By now, fully in the shadow of the gallows, Stephen was loudly proclaiming his innocence to anyone who would listen.

But—we might ask—if he was innocent, why had he confessed? Even now, under retrospective analysis, his motives are not clear. Perhaps interrogation methods were not as humane as they are presumed to be today. Or perhaps Stephen was led to believe the case against him was airtight, so it didn't matter that he was innocent. And cooperation, in the form of a confession, would win him a life sentence instead of a hanging.

But if that's what he believed, he was wrong. The death sentence was passed; Stephen Boorn was doomed.

Was the situation hopeless? Wasn't there anything he could he do?

"The only chance I see," Stephen said, "could be Colvin's alive somewhere. Why don't we advertise for him in the papers?" Perhaps believing they were grasping at straws, the desperate family placed advertisements in the *Rutland Herald* and the *New York Post*. They ran on November 25, 1819.

One can hardly imagine the surprise, shock and horror when—on December 22, 1819—the resurrected Russell Colvin stepped off a stagecoach in Manchester.

The newspaper advertisement had provoked a chain of events that involved tremendous luck and amazing coincidence. When the ad was spotted by a New Yorker named Tabor Chadwick, he recalled a friend's farmhand in New Jersey—a farmhand who not only fit the description, but also answered to the name of Russell Colvin!

Upon his return to Manchester, Colvin faced his supposed murderer. Noting that Stephen Boorn was in chains, Colvin asked, "What is that for?"

Stephen replied, "Because they say I murdered you."

"Why, pshaw," Colvin is said to have explained, "I ain't murdered. Jesse threw a shoe at me once, but it didn't hurt me any."

However, this was not the end of the story.

The Boorn boys were released. Colvin headed back to New Jersey, but uncertainty remained, for the solution to one mystery only created another.

In his fascinating book *The Counterfeit Man*, Gerald McFarland argues that the returning Colvin, like the renowned Martin Guerre, was in reality a clever look-alike impostor—a hired player in a brilliant jailbreak scheme, engineered, most probably, by the boys' father.

It may well be so. The evidence is strong in its favor. But we'll never know for sure. All we can say is that if the returned man was in fact Russell Colvin, so much for the credibility of ghosts as witnesses and supernatural dreams as evidence.

And perhaps more important: Vermont laws regarding *corpus delicti*—proof of murder—were subsequently changed so there can never be such a chain of events again.

Dream Lake

THE PECULIAR CASE OF MANCHESTER'S STEPHEN AND JESSE BOORN is not the only Vermont murder involving a "psychic dream." In the mid-1800s, another murderer was revealed and brought to justice through similar nighttime intuition. This time, the sinister deed took place not on Vermont soil but on Vermont water. The scene of the crime was Fairfield Pond.

In the last century, Stephen Marvin and his wife, Sapho, owned a farm on the shore of Fairfield Pond, about two and a half miles outside of Sheldon. The Marvins also owned a sawmill. Between these two enterprises, they employed a fair number of men. Among them was a young father named Eugene Clifford.

The Cliffords lived near the Marvins, and the two couples were on friendly terms. Mrs. Clifford, her baby in arms, went to visit Mrs. Marvin almost every day. Mrs. Clifford seemed exceptionally proud of two identical paisley shawls that she owned. Whenever she called on Mrs. Marvin, she'd be wearing one shawl, her baby would be wrapped in the other.

One Sunday morning in 1842, Eugene Clifford, along with his wife and child, appeared at the Marvin farm. As usual, Mrs. Clifford and the baby were wearing their look-alike shawls. Clifford had a favor to ask. They'd been invited to Sunday dinner at the home of Mrs. Clifford's parents who lived directly across the lake. The fastest, most direct way to get there was to row. "I'm wondering if we might borrow your rowboat?" Clifford asked.

"Why sure," Stephen Marvin said, "help yourself."

So the Cliffords headed off for the boat while the Marvins headed off to church.

Much later that afternoon, a distraught-looking Eugene Clifford reappeared at the Marvins' farmhouse.

Sobbing and sighing, he choked out the story of how, while crossing the lake, the boat had capsized. In spite of his efforts to save them, his wife and their little baby had drowned.

In the early evening hours, the two bodies were recovered from Fairfield Pond.

The Marvins accompanied the shaken Clifford when he was called to identify his loved ones. While viewing the bodies, Mrs. Marvin noticed that the twin shawls were missing.

She pondered the sight for hours, later remarking to her husband that Mrs. Clifford's corpse looked as if she'd put up quite a struggle to save her life.

A night or two after the drownings, Mrs. Sapho Marvin experienced an especially vivid dream, a dream that repeated itself night after night. It was always the same: she saw Eugene Clifford, all by himself, holding the twin shawls. Balling them up and bundling them tightly to his chest, Clifford took the shawls into a wooded swampland on the shore of the lake.

As the dream progressed, Mrs. Marvin invisibly followed Clifford as he made his way deeper and deeper into the swamp. She saw him walk past a tree that had blown over, its earth-encased root system exposed. Beyond this she clearly saw a hollow stump. Mrs. Marvin watched as Clifford rushed to the stump, then crammed the shawls into its hollow interior. That done, he concealed them beneath a flat stone.

The dream was so real that Sapho Marvin felt as if she'd actually been in that swamp with Eugene Clifford.

One morning, after the dream had repeated itself in an especially lifelike manner, Mrs. Marvin summoned one of her more trusted hired men and asked him to accompany her into the swamp.

Though she had never set foot in this murky marshland before, it all seemed perfectly familiar—the surroundings were exactly as they had appeared in her dream. She felt so acquainted with the terrain that she took the lead as the pair plunged deeper into the marsh.

There, just ahead, she saw the fallen tree with the exposed roots.

And beyond it—the stump!

Who knows what thoughts seared through Mrs. Marvin's mind as she approached the stump? How must she have felt as she slid the flat stone off and peered inside? What kind of dread stabbed at her when she saw, packed into the hollow trunk, the twin shawls once worn by the drowned mother and murdered child?

Mrs. Marvin and the hired hand hurried back to the farmhouse so they could send for the authorities. When the officers arrived, she gave them precise directions to the spot from which they recovered the telltale shawls. Sapho Marvin was the principal witness at Eugene Clifford's trial. Without her testimony the crime might have gone undiscovered and a murderer might have gone free. Without her dream, there would have been no testimony.

Is it any wonder that ever since that day residents of the area have referred to Fairfield Pond by another name?

They call it . . . "Dream Lake."

Sleeping Lucy

No one could be more of a "real Vermonter" than Lucy Ainsworth. She was born in 1819 to a poor family on a struggling hill farm at the edge of Calais. But Lucy acquired a particular "wild talent" that would bring her to the attention of not only her neighbors, but to all of Vermont, all of the United States and eventually much of the world.

History records that Lucy was "a mite peculiar" even as a child. Among her eccentricities was a psychic gift that appeared spontaneously in the spring of 1833 when a neighbor, Nathan Barnes, said he'd lost his gold watch. Lucy and her mother helped the family search, but no one could locate the missing timepiece. After a while, Lucy gave up and went home.

There, feeling strangely tired, she curled up on the sofa and took a nap. When she woke up she excitedly told her mother, "I had a dream! Mr. Barnes's watch is in the tall grass under the hammock near his pear tree. He dropped it while he was asleep."

Sure enough, they found the watch exactly where Lucy said it would be.

Following a few similar demonstrations, skeptical neighbors became convinced of Lucy's ability. With their enthusiastic endorsements, word of her strange abilities spread. Soon people were coming from all around to take advantage of Lucy Ainsworth's "second sight."

A man named Kent from Montpelier drove to Calais to ask Lucy's help finding his billfold with over $300 in it. In a trance, Lucy said the billfold was in somebody's pocket.

"Whose pocket?" Mr. Kent asked, suspecting a thief.

But no, not a thief. Lucy said she saw the pants hanging in somebody's closet; she didn't know whose. But when she described the closet, Mr. Barnes realized that it was his own. He had absent-mindedly changed his pants but forgot to transfer his wallet.

A few years later, things got infinitely stranger. It started when Lucy fell victim to a devastating but undiagnosed illness.

The young woman lost strength, took to her bed and remained sick for more than two years. During the last six months, when she slipped into a kind of "coma," doctors gave up hope.

Her family summoned her favorite brother, Luther, from his home in upstate New York. Luther prayed intensely at Lucy's bedside, almost willing his comatose sister to recover.

Then, something happened. The "why" of the events remains a mystery, but history tells us that Lucy suddenly spoke loudly in her sleep. In a strangely altered voice she said, "I will get well if you will get what I tell you and give it to me." She went on to list some herbs and roots; then she described a method to prepare them.

Where this medical knowledge came from may never be known. All we know is that her family, after some deliberation, decided they had nothing to lose. They mixed-up the concoction, gave it to her, and . . . she got well.

In response to the apparent miracle recovery, Lucy decided to devote the rest of her life to studying the cause and cure of diseases. But apparently her near-death experienced awakened another psychic gift: Lucy discovered that not only had she healed herself, but she could heal other people as well.

Oddly, this new found ability, like her old talent for finding things, depended upon one common condition: she had to be asleep to use the gifts. Consequently, she became known as "Sleeping Lucy."

When she was 21 years old, Lucy married Charles Cooke of Morristown. With his help, her abilities strengthened. By using hypnosis—then called "mesmeric sleep"—Charles was able to encourage a deeper trance. They found the strength of her powers increased as her trance grew deeper. Now Lucy was able to set and sometimes heal broken bones, a rare gift among psychic healers.

The couple moved south to Reading where Lucy devoted all her powers to diagnosing and treating illnesses.

As always, her method was to go into a deep sleep. Only then could she diagnose the illness and describe the components for a remedy. Charles, acting as her assistant, would write down the formula since Lucy was unable to remember anything upon waking. When she woke from her trance, she'd read the prescription and prepare the mixture. (Lucy's life and career resemble that of Edgar Cayce, a more modern healer. Lamentably, while Cayce's cures were recorded and catalogued, no one has yet been able to track down a single one of Lucy's prescriptions.)

In addition to tending local patients, Lucy ran a worldwide medicine-by-mail business. Her remedies—composed of barks, roots and herbs—always seemed to work. Her success angered her more traditional medical counterparts who were treating illness by bloodletting, blistering and prescribing dangerous drugs such as mercury and laudanum.

When Charles Cooke died in 1855, Lucy moved her practice to Montpelier. Her farm on the East Montpelier Road became known as the "Sleeping Lucy Place."

There, a Mr. Everett Raddin became her secretary. In 1876, she and Raddin moved to North Cambridge, Massachusetts, and got married. Together they set up a popular practice, first on Forest Street and later on East Liberty.

In her 53 years of practice, Lucy Ainsworth Cooke is said to have been consulted by well over 200,000 people, from all ranks of society. Due to her remarkable paranormal abilities, Vermont's "Sleeping Lucy"—called Dr. Cooke by many—became known as "the greatest medical clairvoyant of the nineteenth century." No one else ever created such a stir as a clairvoyant and psychic healer or cured as many patients.

Unfortunately, her new husband proved to be a bit of a spendthrift. Unknown to Lucy, Everett squandered much of their money. When he died, he left Lucy deeply in debt.

In 1895, Lucy fell ill. Her daughter, Julia, nursed her, prayed and waited for her sleeping mother to raise her voice and prescribe her own cure.

But Sleeping Lucy remained silent until finally—at age 76—she fell asleep for the last time.

Danville's Divine Comedy

People who are curious about near-death experiences and UFO abductions should consider the strange events that befell John P. Weeks of North Danville back in July of 1838. It is a story townspeople still swear is true. In fact, a verifying document exists, written in Weeks's own hand. It bears the signatures of thirty-one Vermonters. Fifteen of them were eyewitnesses, including four church deacons, three ministers and three medical doctors.

John P. Weeks was a 26-year-old man who lived on a farm in the town's Tampico neighborhood. In the high heat of that fatal summer, Weeks took sick with a dreadfully painful and usually fatal disease, diagnosed as "inflammation of the bowels."

The pain Mr. Weeks experienced was nearly unbearable. For six days, his agony continued. His wife, relatives, and friends wept helplessly at his bedside. Doctors tried unsuccessfully to ease his torment while holy men prayed for his soul.

On Saturday, the sixth day of his ordeal, everyone gave up hope.

They watched powerlessly as John P. Weeks closed his eyes and faded into unconsciousness.

At last the stillness of death settled over him.

After the doctor gave Weeks's family the bad news, his relatives began the process of "laying him out." Some heated water to wash his body; others began removing his clothing.

All of a sudden John sat up in bed and called for his trousers!

Before the startled and unbelieving eyes of the mourners, the dead man jumped out of bed. Then he walked unsteadily to the door where he stood transfixed. He seemed to be watching something no one else could see.

In time, Mr. Weeks recovered completely from his illness. He survived two wives, fathered fifteen children and lived to the age of 70.

Over the years, he told time and again the story of the miracle in which he had participated. He even wrote a narrative account describing all the things that happened to him in those moments between the time the doctor pronounced him dead and the moment he sat up and demanded his pants.

He wrote that while he lay near death, "I looked towards the east door of the house and saw a great reflection of light . . . lighter than the sun. I then saw two angels advancing toward me, and the nearer they came, the brighter they shone. . . . One of them touched me with his finger and my spirit left my body. . . . The other angel sat and watched over my body while my spirit was absent from it. . . . One of the angels left the house and I followed him, floating in a path of light."

Weeks said that when he looked at his own spirit he saw no flesh or blood, yet his spirit was formed in the shape of his body.

As if he were some Yankee version of Dante, Weeks followed his angelic guide through a shadowy, sinister region. He wrote, "I saw a multitude that no man could number, in a dark, lost condition. They were weeping and wailing and trying to climb out of this place, only to fall back again."

Then Weeks ascended a bright and glorious path about three feet wide, to the land of Paradise. He describes Heaven as only a Vermont farmer might: "The land of Paradise is perfectly level, grass perhaps

half an inch high, no trees nor stumps nor stones." He also said the "climate was delightful" and the air was "always agreeable."

The layout of Heaven seems to resemble that of a typical Vermont town. In the same way there's a Danville, a North Danville, West Danville and South Danville, Weeks's Heaven is similarly subdivided.

He described a "Second Heaven" that lies to the east of Paradise. East Heaven is filled with genderless angels singing songs of praise. And, he said, there's even a "Third Heaven" visible from Paradise. Mostly it's made up of God's golden throne (". . . ten thousand times brighter than the brightest gold") and more singing angels.

Weeks wanted to stay in Paradise, but, alas, his work on Earth was not finished. As he was led back to North Danville, they detoured through Hell again, to give him a second glimpse as a reminder. The angel asked John to be sure to warn all sinners not to come to that place of torment. When John agreed, they headed directly back to Earth.

There they found the second angel still watching over John's lifeless body. The angel touched John's body three times and his spirit returned to it. The sensation, John said, was like entering an icy cold room.

And that was the exact moment John P. Weeks sat up and demanded his pants.

He then rose and walked haltingly to the door, following the two departing angels. They paused at the threshold long enough to promise him he'd get completely well. Weeks recovered—just as the angels promised. And he kept his promise to them. He spent the rest of his life telling people about his tour of Heaven and Hell and warning sinners about the hot and hopeless place he had seen on his way to and from Paradise.

Dream or reality? To John P. Weeks the experience was every bit as real as the sickness that brought it about. It changed his life, providing a calling for his remaining 44 years.

I suspect the next time he died, he bypassed the hopeless regions altogether and climbed directly to his little farmhouse on the outskirts of North Heaven.

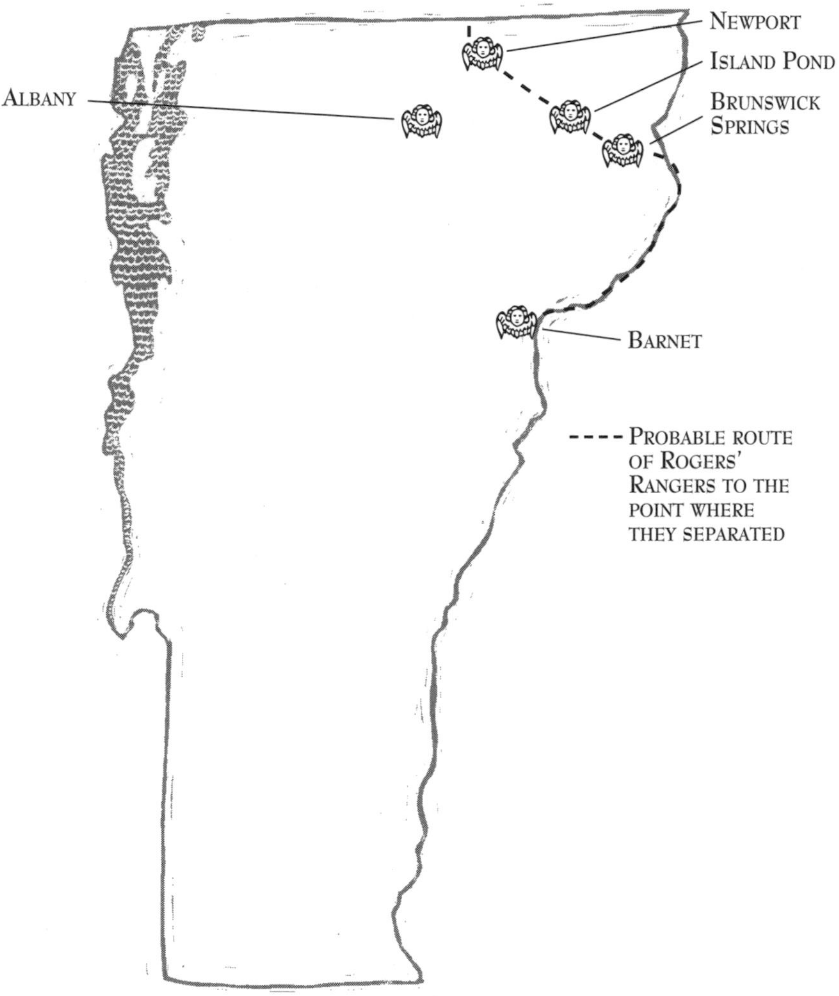

Newport
Island Pond
Albany
Brunswick Springs
Barnet

Probable route of Rogers' Rangers to the point where they separated

CURSES!

VERMONTERS CURSE ALL THE TIME. But a clever profanity uttered by some taciturn old Yankee is usually more humorous than menacing. However, sinister curses *have* been uttered in Vermont, curses intended to invoke evil, injury or total destruction against other people. Such profane condemnation has long been part of the weaponry wielded by priests, magicians, shamans and sometimes ordinary civilian ill-wishers.

Curses seem to be prevalent in almost every culture. They can be used politically, as in the hands of Haiti's "Papa Doc" Duvalier, or for religious retribution, as in the terrifying "Rod of Light" occasionally invoked by certain orthodox Jewish sects. Even the Church of England has its commination service containing twelve curses (with lots of room for extemporization!).

The question here, of course, is do curses work *in Vermont*?

The best answer seems to be: Yes, sometimes. And especially when uttered by Indians.

The Silver Idol

In September of 1759, an elite force of 140 commandos attached to the army of Sir Jeffrey Amherst set out from Crown Point on a secret retaliatory expedition.

Thoroughly experienced in Indian warfare, and familiar with almost every hardship, the formidable body of rangers followed Major Robert Rogers northward for twenty-two days. They pressed on until they surrounded the Indian village of St. Francis, Quebec, about halfway between Montreal and Quebec City, where the St. Francis River meets the St. Lawrence. Silently, under the cover of darkness and without alerting the sleeping villagers, the attack force took positions around the fifty or so Indian dwellings that encircled the Catholic chapel.

At first light on October 4, the Rangers attacked, completely surprising their prey; the only warning was a barrage of lethal gunfire. Villagers who rushed outside were cut down in their tracks. Those who plunged into the river hoping to escape were picked off by sharpshooters. Infants and the aged, males and females, all were slaughtered with equal savagery.

The butchery lasted an incredible two hours. By 7:00 in the morning it was all quiet but for the moans of the dying.

As several of the panic-stricken Abenakis ran into the chapel, they were pursued by a dozen Rangers. The priest stood up to the invaders as terrified Indians cowered behind him. Raising the host, he thundered, "To your knees, monsters! To your knees!"

A Ranger named Bradley shot the priest; the others opened fire on the Abenakis. In about ten minutes, the chapel was full of corpses.

Then the Rangers began to pilfer.

Someone dashed the host to the ground; the rest stripped the altar, stealing anything of value. Their most precious acquisition was a silver statue of the Blessed Virgin Mary.

But the looters froze when an unearthly voice spoke from somewhere amid the piles of corpses. The exact words, spoken in English, were not recorded, nor do we know for certain who uttered them—but a curse was placed on the invaders. In substance, the voice said, "The

Great Spirit will scatter darkness in your path. Hunger will walk before you and Death will strike your tail. Your wives will weep for the dead who will not return."

The invaders paid little attention, demonstrating their scorn by torching the chapel. Then they set fire to the rest of the village.

But apparently the supernatural events had already begun. As the Rangers began to depart, the bell in the chapel started to ring. Immobile with dread, they listened to the slow, measured strokes until the flaming belfry collapsed and the bell clanged to the ground and was silent.

Though only one of their number was killed, Major Rogers realized that separation would offer the best hope of successful retreat. He divided his 139 men into several parties: smaller groups could move faster, and it would be easier for them to acquire game.

He ordered them to rendezvous over on the Connecticut River at the mouth of the Passumpsic River, near present-day East Barnet.

Bradley the priest-killer and eight other Rangers bearing the pilfered silver image headed south through Vermont. Snows and freezing temperatures made progress difficult. Fear of pursuing Indians kept them from stopping long enough to get food. Hunger quickly set in—just as the ominous voice had predicted.

They often thought about relieving themselves of the heavy silver burden, but such wealth was difficult to part with. The statue passed from hand to hand as one after another of the men fell away from exhaustion and died.

Half-crazed with hunger and fatigue, only four emaciated survivors made it to the Connecticut River. Somehow, they had missed the spot where they were supposed to rendezvous with their comrades. Detecting no sign of other survivors, the four presumed they were the only ones to make it safely back from the raid.

Frightened and disheartened, they continued pushing forth, but history has lost their trail. Perhaps they divided again, with some heading west through the Green Mountains. Or maybe they all made for the White Mountains to the east.

They staggered on for days without sustenance, full of despair. They plodded, crept, at last they crawled on their bellies until madness possessed them in the frozen isolation of impenetrable mountains.

The inevitable end wasn't long in coming.

Our unhappy tale concludes with insanity, cannibalism and lonely death. Only one of the original nine survived the ordeal. The rest, including Bradley, perished miserably, perhaps with the words of the curse ringing in their ears. For indeed darkness had scattered their path; hunger had walked before them and Death had inexorably struck them down.

We can be sure that somewhere along their fatal trek, a discarded silver statue—carefully hidden or blasphemously hurled away—awaits some treasure hunter or unwary hiker.

Mercie Dale's Curse

In the town of Albany, on Route 14 near the Black River, there stands a red-brick mansion, Victorian-Colonial in design, built just before the Civil War. In its day, it was a conspicuous show of wealth. And even now—though beautifully restored—it seems somehow out of place, inspiring questions about who could have built such a house? Why in Albany? And what strange secrets might such a place conceal?

As long as the house stands it will be a reminder of one of Vermont's most dramatic run-ins with the supernatural, for the story of Hayden House is the story of a family's destruction, and of a curse, articulated in anger, that took three generations to run its unalterable course.

It all started in 1806, when William Hayden, his wife, Silence, and mother-in-law, Mercie Dale, moved to Lutterloh, Vermont, as Albany was then called. Mercie Dale, a wealthy widow, helped the young couple in many ways, especially financially, making possible the purchase of a house and land. William Hayden quickly proved himself a clever and ambitious businessman. He was active in town politics, ranked captain in the militia, and he owned a public house and a textile mill. As his enterprises expanded, Hayden bought up more and more land.

At some point around 1823, Hayden's greed for land placed him in financial difficulty. He asked his mother-in-law for another loan. But Mercie hesitated, for Hayden had never repaid the loans she'd already given him.

He hounded her so much that she fell ill, eventually coming to believe her son-in-law had poisoned her. Things got so bad that she moved out.

Mercie took a room in the safety of a friend's house, but her illness was not to abate. Even as her health deteriorated, Mercie would have her revenge. In spite of her daughter's marriage to William, she put a curse on the Hayden family. She said, "The Hayden name shall die in the third generation, and the last to bear the name shall die in poverty."

Exactly what empowered the dying woman to make such a curse and why she chose to defer its effects for three generations is not known. Presumably she wanted to spare her daughter immediate discomfort while making William's future as bleak as possible.

Anyway, after Mercie died, William Hayden's financial troubles got worse. A barrage of lawsuits eventually cost him everything. To escape his creditors, he moved to Canada. Later he settled in New York where he died a poor and broken man. Though Hayden had fathered five sons, Mercie Dale's curse was working—for only one son survived to manhood.

William Junior, known as Will, stayed on in Albany where he married a local woman and fathered five children of his own—but only one was male.

Will was enterprising enough to try his hand at railroad building at just the right time. His contracts took him far from Albany, perhaps out of reach of the curse. In any event, Will prospered; he earned a fortune in the railroad business. And that fortune permitted him to start building the grand Hayden Mansion in 1854.

But when he took up residence, things started to go wrong. He had a falling out with his wife over the attentions paid to her by another man. His only son, Henry, began acting strange, often seeming quite unstable. One daughter passed away; he lost another to madness. And his only grandson died at age 5.

To top it all off, Will's eyesight started to go bad, putting an end to his work life. Still, he witnessed the eroding of his fortune.

At the point of Will's death, two generations of Haydens had fallen. Now Will's unstable son Henry remained—the only third generation male and the final target of Mercie Dale's curse.

It is not clear whether Henry tried to save or steal the family fortune, but his strange financial shenanigans so alienated his mother that she cut him out of her will. He kept up the appearance of prosperity by raising cows, racing horses and quite possibly by smuggling Chinese laborers. It is certain that Henry made various efforts to pry money out of the estate—which remained unsettled until after his death by cerebral hemorrhage in 1910.

When Henry died, there was only one Hayden left alive, his daughter, Mamie. All she inherited of the once vast holdings was a bunch of bad debts. Humiliated, unmarried and sickly, she moved to Maine where she died in 1927, poverty-stricken and alone.

With no living heirs to take over, the Hayden mansion was shut up for years. Like its former inhabitants, the old house slowly fell into ruin. Some say that ghosts walked in its chilly, dark hallways. If that is so, then they are the only Haydens to survive the damning words of Mercie Dale's curse.

Waters of Fire

Ripley's Believe It or Not proclaimed the Brunswick Mineral Springs, "The Eighth Wonder of the World." But today it's almost forgotten, hidden away in the most remote, least populated region of Vermont—the fabled Northeast Kingdom. Even the locals can't seem to recall exactly what happened there: something about miracles and preternatural fire and the words of an ancient Indian curse.

But it's all for real. The destruction is a matter of record. Postcards, pieces of china, bottles and obscure memorabilia gather dust on collectors' shelves. And the magical waters still flow, just as they have for thousands upon thousands of years, leaving their oddly American mineral trail of red, white and blue stains.

And then there are the stories . . .

The Brunswick Mineral Springs are a geological anomaly, a strange hybrid of natural beauty, modern mystery and ancient magic.

Ripley deemed the six springs a "wonder" because they all flow from a single knoll, forming a semicircle of about 15 feet. Though nearly as close together as spigots on a soda fountain, the mineral content of each is completely different from that of its neighbor. Moving left to right they are: iron, calcium, magnesium, white sulfur, bromide and—if you are brave enough—arsenic. The springs flow from a steep bank below the crest of a hill, not far from the Connecticut River.

Long before the springs came to Ripley's attention, Native Americans from all over the region knew of their miraculous curative properties. To them, the springs were "Medicine Waters of the Great Spirit," a precious gift to be shared.

The first recorded miracle happened in 1784. Indians from around Lake Memphremagog transported a wounded British soldier to the springs. His arm was so badly damaged that he was in danger of losing it to infection. The shaman held the soldier under the "Medicine Waters," positioning the stricken limb so the mineral streams would converge according to some long-forgotten formula. The ritual and proper application of magic are lost too. But history records one thing for sure—life returned to the damaged arm!

The specifics of what transpired at Brunswick Springs over the next hundred years are pretty vague. We can guess that as more settlers arrived, the notion of free sharing began to erode, to be eventually replaced by free enterprise. Predictably, Colonial businessmen saw financial opportunity in the waters. Native Americans refused to sell what nature gave for free.

Tension led to fighting, and two Indians were killed. The mother of one, a sorceress, uttered enigmatic words, "Any use of the waters of the Great Spirit for profit *will never prosper*." Whether these words were a reminder, a warning or a curse, they would echo ominously for centuries, though their full impact would be slow in coming.

Indian lands were quickly lost while the reputation of the marvelous springs continued to grow.

In 1790, a Major French opened a boarding house to provide travelers with convenient access to the springs. He charged for meals and lodging, but the use of the waters remained free to all.

In 1800, David Hyde turned his home into a sort of Bed, Breakfast and Bath establishment. The enterprise did so well, Hyde was able to expand in 1815. Hyde prospered, but only as an innkeeper; he didn't sell the waters.

By 1820, twelve neighboring families got in on the act, opening their own boarding houses.

Still the Great Spirit's miracle waters remained free for the taking. And their fame increased. They became renowned for curing such exotic ailments as dyspepsia, scrofula, salt rheum, lifeless limbs and loss of vitality. Their ability to relieve kidney problems, consumption, rheumatism and glandular troubles was legendary.

By 1845, travelers were making the difficult journey by stage, horse and on foot from as far away as Portland, Maine, to sample Vermont's healing waters.

Then, in the mid-1800s, something happened that changed the economic face of Vermont. Railroads spread their iron arteries throughout the state making trips to the springs almost effortless. In 1860, accommodations for travelers changed from rustic to regal when Charles Bailey built a hotel near the springs. He quickly sold it at a tidy profit to a dentist named D.C. Rowell. Dr. Rowell christened the place "The Brunswick Spring House" and, year after year, watched its rooms fill to capacity.

Fate seemed to smile on Dr. Rowell. Mineral waters were growing in popularity everywhere, fast becoming the toast of Europe and the U.S.A. Surely Rowell had been in the right place at the right time.

Or so he thought.

Eventually, the enterprising doctor made a fatal mistake; he opened a bottling plant. For the first time, the waters were for sale.

Perhaps the Great Spirit knew that the end had come, that the waters would be forever lost to all but the wealthy.

In 1894, the hotel burned to the ground.

Determined, Rowell rebuilt, calling his new operation "Pine Crest Lodge." Any misfortunes that befell him are unrecorded, so we must conclude that he prospered until he died in 1910.

Now, with the twentieth century up and running, the hotel was for sale again. After 100 years—with nothing to look forward to but more exploitation—the Great Spirit, it seems, had had enough. The countdown began; the worst collision with the supernatural was about to occur.

John C. Hutchins of nearby North Stratford, New Hampshire, looked at the springs and saw a gold mine. He knew that all over the world, resorts were prospering solely because of their weird-tasting water. But this was something special. The Brunswick Springs were a beautiful picture framed by the Connecticut River, the magnificent White Mountains, a tiny sparkling lake and the lovely Green Mountains.

With Robert Ripley providing international promotion, and with the railroad supplying transportation for hordes of health-seekers, how could he possibly lose?

John C. Hutchins bought the place.

Then on September 19, 1929, the hotel burned to the ground!

But of course it was nothing but a freak accident. It had to be. And John C. Hutchins was never one to give up, not when he could turn misfortune into opportunity. He decided to replace the ruins with a bigger and better resort—a grand hotel! A showpiece!

A local contractor with the unlikely name of Harry Savage worked his crew throughout the long, harsh winter months. A true Yankee, Savage was as good as his word; he had the new hotel ready to open its doors by springtime.

What a place it was! Four-and-a-half stories high, a hundred rooms, huge plate glass windows and a 155-foot terrace offering spectacular panoramic views of the Green Mountain splendor.

A staff was hired, including chauffeurs for the two brand-new Packard limousines purchased solely to drive guests to and from the railroad station.

Reservations poured in.

On May 15, 1930—just one month before the hotel was to open—the night watchman spotted smoke billowing from a storage room. Before he could run and call for help, the heated phone lines snapped, cutting him off from the rest of the world.

Flames raged through the rooms like hordes of angry demons. By midday, it was over. The corpse of Hutchins's grand hotel was nothing but a skeleton of twisted pipes and smoldering timbers.

But if the Great Spirit was trying to tell him something, John C.

Hutchins wasn't ready to listen. Two fires in two years were not enough to discourage him. No problem! The determined Hutchins would build again.

Contractor Savage's crew was in practice, so the new hotel went up easily. Again they worked through the winter. By spring of 1931, Hutchins's new hotel was ready for business.

The new building had a few more rooms than its predecessor. More than half of them had private baths. And Brunswick Spring water was pumped into every one.

The exterior design was the same, but with the stucco finish currently in vogue.

The only thing Hutchins had forgotten was the old Indian woman's warning: "Any use of the waters of the Great Spirit for profit will never prosper."

On April 23, 1931, John C. Hutchins's third hotel burned to the ground.

Apparently this time he got the message. Maybe he even became a believer. In any event, he never tried again.

And in the sixty years that have followed, neither has anyone else.

Today there isn't much left of the place. Strange legends of fire and water have faded from memory. But stories are still told of eerie things that have happened there: men have hanged themselves on the grounds; a woman drove her car into the lake and drowned; the body of an infant was found strangled to death.

And people still claim that at night you can see the ghosts of the murdered Indians overlooking the waters or stalking silently across the surface of the lake.

Maybe. Who can say?

All we know for sure is that the magical waters of Brunswick Springs continue to run, spreading their red, white and blue trail across an odd bit of American history.

And, just as the sorceress predicted, no one has ever profited from them for any length of time.

Perhaps today a balance is restored, for the "Waters of the Great Spirit" are once again flowing free.

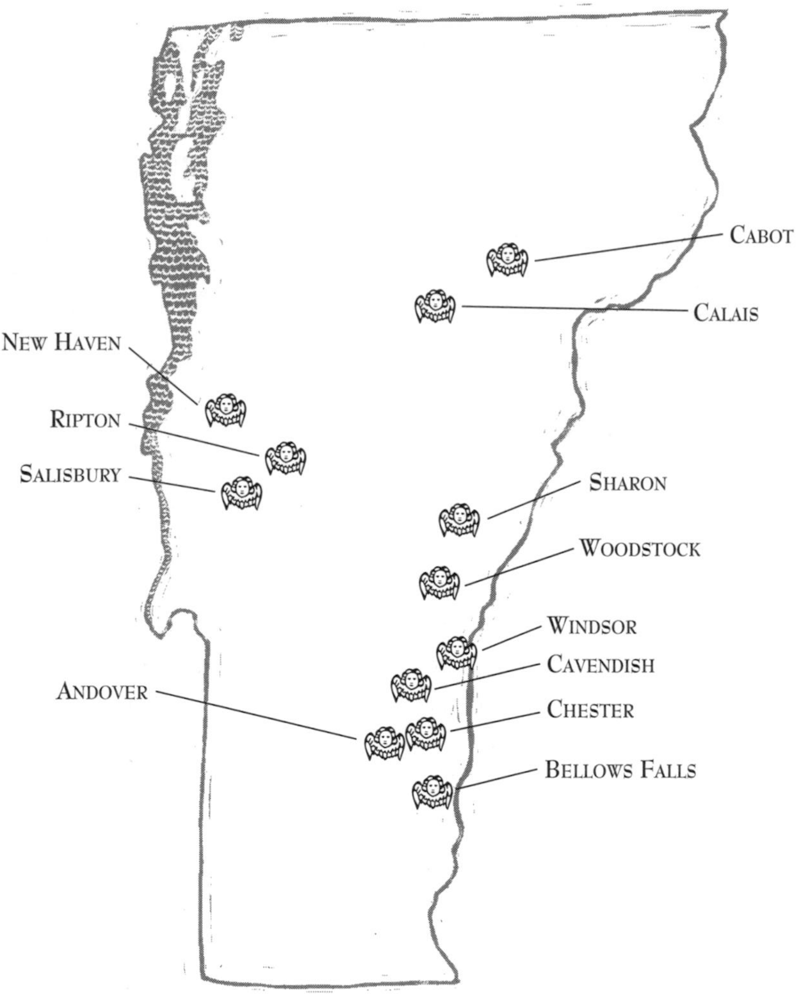

Cabot
Calais
New Haven
Ripton
Salisbury
Sharon
Woodstock
Windsor
Cavendish
Andover
Chester
Bellows Falls

The Vermont Character

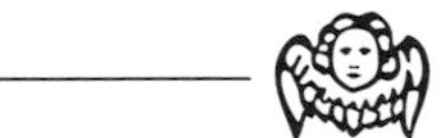

A Vermont character is different from a Maine character or a Pennsylvania character or any other character. A Vermont character is unique, but it's difficult to explain just how.

For one thing, the singular environmental and human climates of Vermont have always tolerated, if not produced, eccentrics. As John Stuart Mill said, "Eccentricity has always abounded when and where strength of character has abounded." I suspect a whole book could be devoted to biographies of the state's oddballs. Simply to list them all would produce a volume much resembling a small town's telephone directory.

Eccentricity often goes hand in hand with genius. Or with extreme individuality. Or, in some cases, with mental disease or damage. Eccentrics can be lovable or loathsome, influential or inconspicuous, tall or short, fat or thin, male or female, Protestant or Catholic. It seems to be an equal-opportunity affliction.

We may not know how to define eccentrics, but we know them when we see them. They might appear impoverished like Pearly Sweat, the hermit of Terrible Mountain in Andover, or as prosperous as Columbus Smith, builder of Salisbury's pseudo-Italianate Shard Villa. They might be misers like Hetty Green, the millionaire witch of Wall Street (and Bellows Falls), whose son lost his leg to gangrene because she couldn't find a free clinic. Or they can be generous like Joseph Battell, who talked to pine trees and who gave his Bread Loaf Inn and thousands of woodland acres to Middlebury College.

They can be amusingly benign like Pardon James of Calais, who wouldn't touch anything, or tremendously influential like Sharon's Joseph Smith, founder of the Mormon religion.

They might be heroes like Ethan Allen, or nearly invisible like a neighbor I remember from my childhood whose house was full of the bottles she'd collected over a lifetime, each filled with a different color liquid.

Since a true Vermont character is so hard to define, perhaps lack of definition is the best definition—the contrary cusses simply won't become part of any generalization.

I have chosen four of my favorite eccentrics for inclusion here.

The last Vermont character in this section is especially important to me simply because he's from my hometown, Chester. He's always been a kind of hero . . .

Zera Colburn: A Calculating Boy

There is a lot more to the town of Cabot than cheeses. Of historical interest, for example, is that it was settled in 1783 by Daniel Webster's uncle Benjamin. The Bayley-Hazen Military Road passes through town. And long before Cabot was known for milk products, it was known for whiskey. Prior to 1832, there were twelve distilleries in this spirited community!

But in terms of historical oddities, nothing can hold a candle to Zera Colburn. Born there in 1804, Zera's bizarre abilities brought him local fame when he was just 6 years old. Later, those same abilities would make him a big cheese all over America and in much of Europe, bringing him to the attention of thousands, from riffraff to royalty.

Abiah Colburn, Zera's father, was a hard-working farmer and carpenter. His biggest fear was that he couldn't continue to support his wife, his seven sons and his two daughters. But his prospects changed in 1810, after Zera's sixth birthday.

Mr. Colburn was building a cabinet. Little Zera sat at his feet, playing contentedly with scraps of wood. Suddenly—strangely—the child began chanting the multiplication tables: "Seven times five is thirty-five. Eight times nine is seventy-two," and so on.

Mr. Colburn was astonished. Why, the lad had only been in school a couple of weeks. Suspecting the numerical song was simply lodged in Zera's memory like a nursery rhyme, Mr. Colburn tried asking a few arithmetic problems. Zera answered the questions perfectly, just as fast as his father could ask them. A neighbor stopped by and confirmed the miracle, then, like a town crier, ran off to spread the news.

Local folks began dropping by to witness Zera's miraculous abilities. Everyone agreed, young Colburn was surely a new wonder of the world!

With that, Mr. Colburn envisioned an end to poverty, a way to escape his dreary life of wood and weeds. If Zera was a true prodigy, why, lots of money could be made exhibiting him. At last there would be better things for himself and his family.

Although they hated to leave their native Cabot, Mr. Colburn and Zera took to the road. Their first stop was Danville, where inquisitors questioned Zera at the courthouse. Leaving the town fathers suitably baffled, the duo pressed on to Montpelier and the state legislature. They continued to Burlington, then on to Dartmouth College in Hanover, New Hampshire. At every stop, panels of intellectuals questioned the boy, but no one could stump him.

Zera also performed before crowds, dazzling everyone with his lightning calculations.

The Colburns headed south to Boston and Harvard College. There, a group of scholars grilled young Zera. One professor demanded disdainfully, "How many seconds in two thousand years?"

Zera squirmed in his seat for a moment, then replied, "Seven hundred thirty thousand *days*. Seventeen million five hundred twenty thousand *hours*. One billion fifty-one million two hundred thousand *minutes*. Sixty-three billion seventy-two million *seconds*."

It took the interrogators quite a while to confirm that Zera was correct. Their next question wasn't posed with such scorn.

After that, father and son toured most big cities on the East Coast, giving amazing demonstrations in packed auditoriums. Then they sailed to Europe, where they'd measure the boy against the mathematical bigwigs in England.

In London, Zera was severely challenged: "Now young man, I'd like you to square eight hundred eighty-eight thousand eight hundred and eighty-eight."

Zera took a breath, thought for less than a minute and replied, "Seven hundred ninety billion one hundred twenty-one million eight hundred seventy-six thousand five hundred and forty-four."

The Englishman glanced at his colleagues who were figuring furiously. Finally, one of them nodded: the answer was correct.

Undaunted, the questioner cleared his throat. "Very good. Now if you will, please multiply that total by forty-nine . . ."

Zera fired back, "Thirty-eight trillion seven hundred fifteen billion, nine hundred seventy-one million, nine hundred fifty thousand six hundred and . . . fifty-six." Correct again.

Leaving this group of dignitaries astounded by his wizardry, Zera and his father crossed the channel to France. There, they happened upon the writer Washington Irving, who was delighted with the boy. He introduced them to other luminaries who were equally impressed. Even Napoleon took an interest in the little Vermonter. A genius himself, Napoleon felt such an extraordinary mind should be trained. He offered Zera a scholarship at the Lyceum Napoleon. He studied there for a short while until he—or maybe his father—became discontent. Perhaps feeling more at home in an English-speaking country, the Colburns returned to London. This time, they secured an introduction to the Earl of Bristol, who awarded Zera a scholarship to the Westminster School.

Zera put in four years, until his father died of tuberculosis. The grieving teenager returned to the United States alone—and made straight for Cabot.

Sadly, his mother and his siblings didn't recognize him after ten long years. Perhaps the stark reality of his impoverished family inspired the end of his career. Zera never exhibited his wild talent again.

Wanting only to help his loved ones, Zera took a teaching job at a college in New York State. He was miserable, unsuccessful and after just a few months, he quit and headed home to Cabot, feeling like a failure.

After unsuccessfully sampling several other positions, Zera became a Methodist preacher, traveling seven different circuits in Vermont. During these years, he married and had three daughters. But added family responsibilities required more money. After ten years of preaching, Zera changed careers again. He put his boyhood travels and European education to good use teaching languages at Norwich University in Norwich, Vermont.

He stayed there for five years. Then, at age 34, Zera Colburn died, an impoverished and bitter young man. In spite of his amazing dexterity with numbers, Zera just couldn't compute the formula for happiness.

Miller's Armageddon

THE APPROACHING MILLENNIUM seems to be inspiring all sorts of oddball spiritual speculation. I've even heard people say the end of the world is coming. But nobody has ever said it with the conviction of William Miller of New Haven, Vermont.

Miller was born in 1782, the oldest of sixteen children. By the time he reached maturity, he'd become a confirmed atheist. But while in the military, he witnessed horrible deaths and such tremendous suffering that he began to reconsider his position. After experiencing a serious leg wound, a head injury and a diseased arm, Miller became a church-goer in 1815. Then he left the military to marry Lucy Smith of Poultney.

The summer of 1816 was the strangest in memory. May and June brought hail, sleet and snow more than a foot deep in places. Ice choked water lines. Summer temperatures remained below 40 for days on end. By the end of August, most of the Green Mountains were snow-covered. Birds died in the trees; new-shorn sheep froze to death. Nothing turned green, and most crops failed.

These tragedies, coupled with the ominous halo around the sun, suggested something weird was taking its course. To understand what, Miller began a fourteen-year period of extensive Bible study. From references in the Book of Daniel and Revelations, he determined that the end of the world was coming. His calculations revealed the approximate date—somewhere from March 21, 1843 to about one year later: March 25, 1844.

Then, in 1832, when William Miller was 50, God spoke to him. God said, "William, tell the world of your findings." Needless to say, Miller didn't argue. He was puzzled though: how could he, a simple farmer, get *any* kind of a message to the whole world?

Immediately, as if by divine intervention, the preacher at the nearby Dresden Baptist Church suddenly fell ill. Miller was invited to preach the sermon. His message of impending doom fascinated and frightened the congregation. "Graves will open," he told them. "Christ will reappear. There will be signs in the heavens. The dead will rise."

He quickly became a popular guest speaker all over New England as unearthly occurrences—earthquakes, visions, revolutions—lent credence to his terrifying message. Perhaps most convincing of all, in early November 1833, a brilliant shower of shooting stars lit up the sky.

For many, that was proof enough. Bibles sold like hotcakes as thousands of people converted to Millerism. Hundreds of preachers helped spread the new prophet's doomsday theology.

As the fatal days approached, people who died were not buried. Instead, they were carried to common areas where they could all ascend together. Girls broke their wedding dates so they could enter Heaven as virgins. One Millerite, a farmer from my hometown of Chester, made "ascension robes" for six of his best cows. "They'll come in mighty handy up there," he said. "It's a long trip and the kids'll be wanting some milk."

Sadly, the most fanatical Millerites actually killed their families and themselves. Misguided but well intentioned, they theorized the dead would be the first to be taken into Heaven.

Then came another sign—the most dramatic of all. The Great Comet of 1843 appeared in the sky. It was the biggest ball of fire ever to approach the Earth, its tail an estimated 200 million miles long. At such a display, even the atheists were trembling. The number of Miller's followers quickly doubled.

The prophet sent out word that he had finally computed the *exact date* the world would end: April 3, 1843.

People from all over the country gave away their homes and belongings and climbed hills to get a head start on their trip to Heaven. Dressed in long white ascension robes, they built huge bonfires, prayed and sang hymns.

But nothing happened.

The impoverished faithful disbanded, reminding each other that the original prophesy had said *between* March 21, 1843 and March 25, 1844. They still could have up to a year to wait.

And wait they did. Tension, fear and apprehension mounted. At last the fatal day—March 25, 1844—came and went with nary a bang nor a whimper.

Meanwhile, busily rechecking his calculations, Miller found his error! He had used the Gregorian calendar instead of the Jewish calendar—he was seven months off. The *real* date of doomsday would be October 22, 1844. This time for sure.

Unbelievable as it sounds, after two failed doomsdays, Millerites rallied again. Converts reached almost a million.

Of course, on October 22 nothing happened.

Bonfires died, hymns fell to silence and confused crowds of homeless robed figures realized they'd lost far more than their possessions. Hospitals and mental asylums did a booming business. A different motivation prompted more suicide and family slaughter.

Miller, who hadn't given anything away, retreated in comparative luxury. No one questioned why—after he'd predicted the end of the world *for certain*—he was making home improvements, filling his woodsheds, stocking his pantry and tending his livestock. He lived in comfortable seclusion until his death in 1849. During his last five years, his eyesight failed along with his reason. Perhaps his vision was miraculously restored on his death bed when he uttered his final words. "Victory, at last," he said. "Look. I see Jesus!"

A Hole in One

I CAN'T SAY HOW MANY TIMES VERMONT has caught the attention of curio collector Robert Ripley, but the terrifying events that happened to Phineas Gage in Cavendish not only made it into *Believe It or Not*, but into serious medical texts as well.

When I was a child in southern Vermont, I heard the story of Phineas Gage from my father and from other people around the village. After all, it happened in the next town. But the facts leading up to the event were always a little hazy. No two stories matched exactly.

Some accounts say Phineas visited a gypsy fortune-teller who made an odd prediction. "You will appear on the stage," she is said to have told him. "And you will become famous. But the icy finger of death will touch you before sunset tomorrow."

Famous? Why, Phineas didn't believe it. He wasn't a performer; he was a railroad man, by God. And the only stage he expected to be on was the one from Cavendish to Rutland! So next day he went to work as usual and thought no more about it.

At just 25 years of age, Phineas was a construction foreman for the Rutland and Burlington Railroad. All accounts describe him as intelligent, reliable, well-balanced and—though he was a demanding boss—well-liked.

On the fateful day, September 13, 1848, Phineas was supervising the blasting of some ledge. The procedure was to drill a hole in the rock, pour in some blasting powder, pack it with sand, then touch it off.

It was easy; he'd done it a thousand times.

After ordering the men to stand clear, Phineas straddled the hole and inserted a three-and-one-half-foot iron crowbar, called a tamping rod, into its opening . . . but something happened.

Perhaps the sand was packed incorrectly. Perhaps the rod scraped against the rock causing a spark. Whatever the reason, the powder ignited. It blasted the rod 50 feet into space like a shell from a cannon. Stone and dust filled the air as the explosion rumbled through the Vermont hills.

When the cloud cleared, Phineas was on the ground. Though whimpering and convulsing, he was alive. As the men rushed to him, they saw he was trying to sit up. It was unbelievable: apparently their boss hadn't even been hurt.

Closer examination showed his clothes and hands were burned. And he was bleeding: the left side of his face and the top of his head were covered with blood. The men tried to stop the hemorrhaging with cloths as they carried Phineas to the nearby Adams Hotel where they got him a room.

Doctor Edward Williams, a former railroad man, quickly arrived on the scene. He was soon joined by another physician, Dr. John Harlow.

At first the doctors thought Phineas had two wounds: one below his left eye, another at the top of his head. But upon closer examination, they grew more and more astounded. What they saw was contrary to all their training, contrary to all logic.

Phineas Gage had suffered but a single wound. Apparently, the crowbar had entered Gage's head below his left eye and was blown completely through his skull!

Cleaning bone fragments from the openings, Dr. Harlow confirmed their unsettling suspicion: he was able to touch the fingers of both hands together inside Gage's head. Yet the man hadn't even been knocked out.

In fact, Phineas Gage was up and walking within the week.

Though he had lost his left eye, he remained physically the same. His memory and high intelligence were intact. But he had changed. Changed so much the railroad wouldn't hire him back.

His conduct had turned impulsive, boisterous, unpredictable. Like a capricious child, he'd swing from rage to tears in a fraction of a second. And, for the first time in his life, he spoke in the grossest profanities. Phineas Gage had survived against all odds, but the cost was high: he'd lost his self-control, his judgement and his ethical sense. Dr. Harlow wrote, "The equilibrium, or balance, between his intellectual faculties and animal propensities seems to have been destroyed."

His friends and acquaintances put it more simply; they said he was no longer Phineas Gage.

Though Gage's story wasn't readily believed by doctors and scientists, P.T. Barnum knew a good thing when he heard it. He hired Gage for his museum in New York City. There the former railroad foreman—and his crowbar—were put on exhibition. Gage was billed as "The Only Living Man with a Hole in His Head." Amazingly, Gage survived another twelve years in this condition.

If there really had been a gypsy fortune-teller, her predictions all came true: The icy finger of death *did* touch Phineas Gage, yet he went on to appear on stage. And yes, he became famous because of his performance.

But one thing can't be argued: Gage's tragedy led to an important discovery for medical science. Prior to that time, linking emotional activity to the geography of the brain was unheard of. Then Gage's accident proved that a physical change in the brain can affect behavior. The 3-foot tamping bar actually severed the connection between two parts of Gage's brain: the frontal cortex, or thinking part, and the limbic region—the emotional part. Consequently, Gage was unable to control his emotions after the blast.

Although Gage would never understand his contribution to medicine, his case is still studied by neuroscientists and medical students all over the world.

And today, the railroad foreman from Cavendish, Vermont, is on exhibit once again. Gage's skull—and the crowbar—are permanently displayed at the Warren Anatomical Medical Museum at Harvard University.

The Phantom and Mr. Adams

ONE SEPTEMBER NIGHT IN 1886, a sixteen-year series of burglaries began with a safe-cracking at the Adams & David Company in Chester. The bizarre nature of this and subsequent crimes—more than fifty in all—baffled the population of 2,000 and created such uneasiness that the little town could no longer be described as "sleepy."

The thefts were strange because of their apparent impossibility. And stranger still because of the odd things that were stolen: a box of bow ties, a bag of doughnuts, roofing shingles, a bicycle, a sack of grain. The phantom burglar didn't confine himself just to oddball items; he took more expensive and conventional things, too, like money and valuables. The crimes were always unpredictable and often seemingly senseless.

What's more, his escapades seemed to demonstrate a perverse contempt for his victims and for the law. He would never take the easy route into a building if a complicated one were available. His actions indicated great strength, agility and, apparently, a sinister, cunning, intelligence. No one, nothing, was safe from Chester's ingenious and eclectic thief. People not used to locking their homes started barring doors and sleeping with weapons beside their beds.

Druggist F.W. Pierce bought a supply of revolvers to sell to frightened citizens, but the phantom broke in and swiped most of them before they were sold.

In response to at least six break-ins at his general store, (now Carpenter's Emporium) James E. Pollard had a Boston company install a fancy burglar-alarm system. As if to mock this high-tech security device, the thief broke in without triggering the alarm, then left with a fur coat, a woman's cape and fifteen dollars. He—or she—had entered through a 14-by-18-inch window, the only one not wired because it was considered too small.

Chester had no police force in those days. The responsibility of fighting crime fell on the shoulders of the constable and town selectmen. They hired a private detective from Boston who proved to be an alcoholic. He was dismissed after effectively uncovering all Chester's sources of illegal booze, but no burglar.

One distinguished town father, First Selectman Clarence Adams, stepped forward and offered reward money from his own pocket. A bachelor with an active mind and a penchant for mystery fiction, Adams joined the hunt for the phantom thief. Perhaps he felt it was his duty as a citizen and selectman, or maybe he longed for a little adventure in such a quiet town. But whatever his reason, he decided to play detective.

And he fit the role perfectly. He was tall, wiry and considered quite handsome with his fine clothes and rakish handlebar mustache. He was well educated, fair-minded, prosperous, and had won the respect of all the townspeople. A selectman, a trustee in the Whiting Library and the Chester Savings Bank, even a member of the Vermont legislature, Adams was the type of gentleman mothers encouraged their sons to emulate.

Not surprisingly, the multi-talented Adams displayed an aptitude for police work. Before long he was more or less running the investigation. He approved security plans, consulted about strategy, even examined crime scenes.

Everyone felt better now that Mr. Adams was on the case.

Charles H. Waterman owned a gristmill (now an art gallery) on the Williams River. The burglar had robbed it several times and Waterman was sick of it. Knowing which window the thief favored, he rigged up an ingenious pulley that would fire a shotgun if someone opened that sash.

Eager to boast about his clever device, Waterman sent for Clarence Adams. But the selectman was away on business.

That night—July 29, 1902—Waterman's son Gardner heard the roar of a single shotgun blast. The boy dashed to fetch his father and together they summoned Constable Henry Bond.

Waterman and his son followed Bond as, gun in hand, he searched the mill's dark interior. They found nothing but sacks of grain and shadows. Then they examined the window. Blood darkened the windowsill and smeared the shards of glass scattered on the floor. But they found no dead burglar.

Later that evening, another shooting was reported. Clarence Adams arrived home around ten, limping and in pain. He explained to Mrs. Elmina Walker, his housekeeper, that he'd been accosted on the road by two highwaymen who'd shot him in the leg.

A friend who was staying at the Adams house, William Dunn, ran to get help. Soon Dr. Walter Havens and Constable Bond arrived to treat the wound and to question the victim. They listened to Adams's story, examined his mutilated leg, checked the crime scene and discovered the first substantial clue about the phantom's identity: the eighty-four pieces of birdshot removed from Adams's leg matched exactly the Number 8 shot from Waterman's gun.

The conclusion, though completely unbelievable, was inescapable: Clarence Adams and Chester's phantom burglar were one and the same.

Armed with a warrant, Constable Bond searched Adams's home. There he discovered evidence of Adams's dark half. His 2,000 volume library was nearly half full of books suggesting his taste for romance and adventure: hundreds of detective stories and works by Arthur Conan Doyle, Poe, even Robert Louis Stevenson's *Doctor Jekyll and Mr. Hyde*. Conspicuous, too, were books on the occult and the works of Anton Mesmer, a pioneer in the science of hypnotism.

They also found boxes of bow ties, bundles of shingles and, hanging in a tree out back, a rusted bicycle.

Adams had no choice but to confess. During his trial in Woodstock, he articulated the nearest thing we'll ever have to a motive for his peculiar crimes. He testified that he had developed both sides of his nature, encouraging the good as well as the bad. It had worked: he'd become the town's leading citizen and its most successful criminal.

On August 14, 1902, the judge sentenced Clarence Adams to the prison at Windsor. He'd be locked up for ten years.

Adams's education, poise and cunning made him an ideal prisoner. He quickly became the prison librarian and somehow charmed Warden E. W. Oakes. Mostly he kept to himself, but he did befriend another inmate, an educated man who'd had some medical training. Adams's new friend worked as an orderly, assisting the prison's consulting physician, Dr. John D. Brewster.

An occasional visitor broke the monotony of Adams's prison life, the most frequent of whom was his good friend William Dunn.

Everything seemed to be going well until February 22, 1904, when Adams took sick. It was the year of a pneumonia epidemic, so Dr. Brewster and his orderly were stretched pretty thin.

Adams's condition worsened every day. He was moved to the prison infirmary and tended by his friend. There, convinced his time would soon be up, Adams requested that Warden Oakes release his remains to William Dunn.

On Friday, February 26, 1904, under the orderly's care, Clarence Adams died. The orderly prepared the death certificate and presented it to Dr. Brewster who, perhaps after a perfunctory reading, signed it. The cause of death: edema of the lungs—pneumonia.

And here the story should end, but it doesn't. In fact, it's at this point the story starts getting really weird.

Because not long after Adams's death, people started seeing him!

A local salesman, John Greenwood, spoke with him in Montreal. A traveler saw him in Nova Scotia. People ran into him out west . . .

Had Chester's phantom burglar somehow returned from the dead?

A lurid but fascinating theory was posed in the Boston papers, then echoed in newspapers all over the world. They argued that Clarence Adams was as clever breaking out of places as he was breaking in. Had he, they asked, engineered a clever escape from jail? If so, how?

Facts and speculation mesh at many points as we try to reconstruct Adams's resurrection and escape. But, unfortunately, for every fact there is a question:

FACT: Clarence Adams was able to hypnotize himself.

Could he have put himself into a hypnotic sleep and passed himself off as dead?

FACT: Prison Doctor Brewster never viewed the corpse.

Did Adams's orderly friend, a co-conspirator, get the death certificate quickly signed by the overworked Dr. Brewster?

FACT: William Dunn, along with a coffin, arrived Saturday morning to claim the body without having been summoned or informed that Adams had died.

Could his arrival have been prearranged?

FACT: Dunn took possession of Adams's remains and helped mortician Lyman Cabot transport the corpse to his Windsor undertaking establishment where it lay unattended all Saturday afternoon.

Is it possible that somewhere between the jail and the embalming process, Adams's body was switched for a cadaver, perhaps obtained from the nearby Dartmouth Medical School?

FACT: On Monday, a casket was transported 25 miles to the Cavendish cemetery.

Who, or what, was in the coffin?

FACT: No family member ever identified the body. But cemetery sexton Henry D. Sanders opened the box two months later and peeked at the corpse. "It looked like Clarence," he said.

But was it? After that amount of time in a box, wouldn't anyone look like Clarence?

FACT: Suddenly, Henry D. Sanders was able to pay off most of his debts.

Isn't the acquisition of this wealth rather oddly timed?

FACT: Reliable witnesses claimed to have seen and talked to Adams in Canada. (And, Adams *did* like to travel.)

FACT: The family never permitted the grave to be opened to determine who—or what—the casket contained.

Why not?

Put these facts and possibilities together and it appears that Adams engineered an ingenious prison escape.

But someone's body remained in the Cavendish vault until the ground was soft enough for it to be buried on May 1, 1904.

Was it Adams? Can we ever find out for sure?

If the coffin were inspected now, almost one hundred years after burial, the condition of the corpse would make identification impossible. And there would be no fingerprints and dental records.

But there is a way to tell.

Although Adams's flesh may be entirely gone, one thing would not decompose: Number 8 shot from the gunshot wound. Wayne Dengler, an investigator for Windham County State's Attorney, and Rick Bates, a superintendent for the Department of Corrections, tell me there is no way Dr. Havens could have removed it all. There would probably be a couple of tablespoonfuls in the casket. Also, Adams's leg bone would be pitted in a telltale manner.

Students of this bizarre bit of Vermontiana often speculate about where Adams found the inspiration for his dark career and puzzling resurrection.

His housekeeper, Mrs. Elmina Walker, thought she knew: "Reading is the cause of it all," she said. "It turned the poor man's head."

A pamphlet from the Chester Historical Society derived from a *Vermont Life* article by Walter Hard and Stephen Greene suggests that Adams's inspiration may have been William Brodie, an eighteenth-century prototype for Stevenson's *Dr. Jekyll and Mr. Hyde*. By day a prosperous and respected Scottish businessman, by night a thieving ne'er-do-well, Brodie was hanged in 1788. Supposedly he conspired with a physician and possibly the hangman, and may have escaped death on the gallows. He was later recognized, so the story goes, strolling the streets of Paris.

In *Vermont Saints and Sinners*, Lee Dana Goodman finds a mentor closer to home. Joseph Burnham of Woodstock may have escaped from the same prison in essentially the same way!

And, considering Adams's interests, it is likely he would have known the story.

In June 1826, Burnham, a 44-year-old farmer, was convicted of rape and sentenced to ten years hard labor at Windsor prison.

His son and many of his friends were Freemasons who rallied to his defense, planning to petition the Governor for a pardon.

But during his fourth month in prison, Joseph Burnham mysteriously died. Three days later, his remains were released to his son for burial.

Then people started seeing him!

Rumors spread that he was living in New York City. In fact, a couple of Woodstock men with the unlikely names of Lyman Mower and Aaron Cutter claimed they had spoken to him there!

Uncertainty grew. On September 29, 1829, the *Woodstock Observer* launched an investigation, raising several interesting questions: How could Burnham's son have received word of his father's death and traveled from Manhattan to Windsor Prison so quickly?

What was the cause of death? No one knew; it wasn't on the death certificate. Worse, the death certificate had disappeared.

If there was a question about the cause of death, why hadn't there been an autopsy?

Pressing harder, they asked prison officials to explain why Burnham's body had been left unattended for several hours in an isolated area before it was moved to the prison hospital.

Speculation ran wild: maybe someone swapped the live Burnham for a look-alike corpse? Could he have faked his illness, then had someone—perhaps his son—slip him a drug that would put him into a deathlike sleep?

Such an escape would have taken money and accomplices.

Conspiracy theorists speculated that the prison warden and doctor were—like Burnham—Freemasons. As members of this secretive fraternal order, they were required to help *any* fellow mason whose life, welfare or liberty was in jeopardy. Joseph Burnham would have been a prime candidate for such assistance.

With state officials implicated, the Vermont General Assembly appointed a commission to investigate Burnham's death and possible escape. The body was dug up—twice—but it had been in the ground for three years and—to speak euphemistically—it was in no shape to be identified.

Prison records showed no indication of foul play, but character checks were another thing entirely. Cutter and Mower appeared less than honorable. Still, they stuck to their story. Mower even offered to produce the living Burnham if an adequate reward were offered.

By this time, the state of Vermont was eager to clear things up. They offered a reward and even promised Burnham a full pardon if he'd just fess-up.

Our tale ends here. A delegation accompanied Mower to New York, but Burnham never showed. On November 10, 1829, several Vermont newspapers published the commission's findings: Joseph Burnham had actually died in Windsor prison.

Maybe it's true. Who knows?

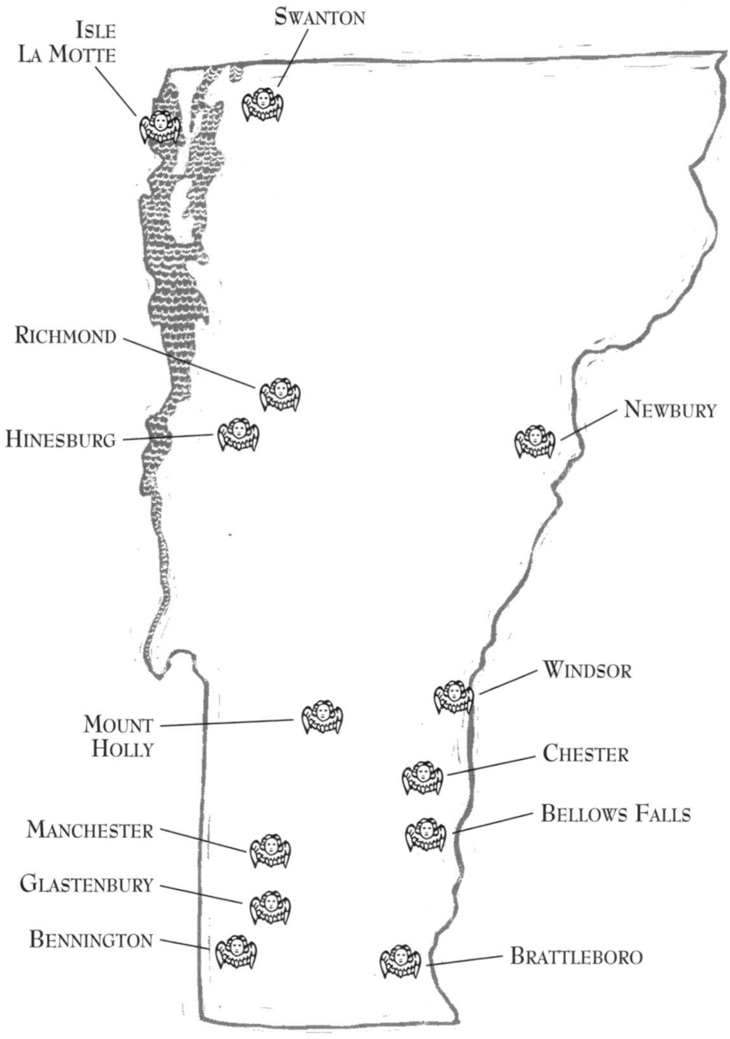

Isle La Motte
Swanton
Richmond
Newbury
Hinesburg
Windsor
Mount Holly
Chester
Bellows Falls
Manchester
Glastenbury
Bennington
Brattleboro

Lingering Mysteries

"Everyone loves a good mystery"—we've heard it said over and over, because it's true! And I hope this book has introduced you to some good ones.

As we've seen, a few have been solved—at least to some degree. Witness the apprehension of Chester's phantom burglar and the mystical identification of the killer at Dream Lake.

Some mysteries remain puzzling: although the fearsome Goonyak has been explained, we still don't have a clue about the identity of Old Slipperyskin.

It's likely we'll eventually discover if giant cats really stalk our forests. And in time I bet we'll be able to classify those evasive submersible specimens that haunt Vermont lakes and rivers.

We may even determine who—or what—electrocuted farmer Ranney's cows.

But perhaps we'll never know the source of those indefinable shapes in the Eddy brothers' farmhouse, or the truth about the odd, seemingly mechanical devices soaring through our skies.

And what of the Granite Monster? Will its whereabouts ever be discovered? The odds are against it.

The following six unsolved mysteries hold a particular fascination, at least for me. For one thing they possess certain bizarre elements that make them especially perplexing. For another, I suspect their solutions would raise a whole string of brand new questions.

Three of them have the potential to change history as we know it. Two would have profound impact on individual lives and reputations. One would give us a whole new look at Vermont's changeable weather.

A list of their titles could easily pass for the contents page from a book of Sherlock Holmes stories:

The Mystery of the Bigfoot Bird
The Mystery of the Puzzling Puddles
The Mystery of the Graye Area
The Mystery of the Copper Seekers
The Mystery of the Deadly Conspirators
The Mystery of the Bennington Triangle

The first of these unsolved mysteries has to do with the strangest footprint I've ever encountered . . .

The Mystery of the Bigfoot Bird

AFTER RESEARCHING CHAMP and some of the other monsters in this book, I got to wondering what sorts of giant animals had actually lived here in prehistoric times. Did dinosaurs once roam the Green Mountain State?

It's hard to tell; the fossil record is distinguished but, unfortunately, all too brief. Tiny Isle La Motte boasts the oldest fossilized coral reef in the world—going back some 400 million years. Woolly mammoths' teeth have been found in Richmond, Brattleboro and Mount Holly, indicating their presence here about 12,000 years ago. And I mustn't forget our official state fossil, the skeleton of a white whale discovered by railroad workers in Charlotte in August 1849.

However, the most dramatic dinosaurs—*Tyrannosaurus rex*, *Triceratops* and the long-necked, vegetable-chomping *Brachiosaurus* didn't live here. The topography was far too mountainous for them.

Jeff Howe, curator of UVM's Perkins Geology Museum, speculates that arctic or alpine dinosaurs might have existed here. But traces of these animals are rare, partly because Vermont's geologic conditions weren't right for preserving dinosaur footprints.

Nonetheless, hundreds of dinosaur footprints have been found nearby. Along the Connecticut River basin, especially around Amherst, Massachusetts, there is ample evidence of dinosaur presence. Some three-toed tracks displayed at Perkins Museum are 150 million years old, made by animals 12 to 15 feet tall!

Okay, that's impressive, but not especially weird or mysterious. But read on . . .

One bit of research led to another until I eventually came across the record of a similar prehistoric paw print that actually *was* found in Vermont. The beast that made it has never been identified, and probably never will be. It was just one single track but that's enough to make it one of Vermont's lingering mysteries.

This curiosity was embedded in a rock that extended into the Connecticut River at Bellows Falls. Its impressive dimensions apparently caused quite a stir in the scientific community at the beginning of the nineteenth century. For years, the three-toed anomaly was a popular tourist attraction. Local folks loved to show it off because it consistently captured the interest of travelers, scientists and journalists, who described it in many different publications.

In his *History of Rockingham*, published in 1907, L. S. Hayes depicts the fossil as ". . . a clearly defined footprint of a huge bird of some unknown species. It was described as an exact reproduction of an exaggerated hen's track and measured"—now get this—"FIVE FEET IN LENGTH."

Five feet! What sort of behemoth bird could leave such a track? I'd hate to run into the prehistoric chicken who made it!

Anyway, this gigantic fossil could have been an especially important scientific find because nothing like it was ever discovered before or since. If it still existed it might have displaced the Charlotte whale as the Vermont State Fossil. Unhappily, this mystery, like so many others involving unknown animals, will never be solved.

Hayes's history continues, "About the year 1800, the faculty of Dartmouth College arranged to secure the curiosity for their museum. A time was set for the removal to Hanover of the section of stone in which it was embedded. Some unappreciative and jealous persons, learning of the plan to remove it, blew the interesting specimen into fragments, with powder, rather than have it taken from the vicinity."

And in so doing they removed it from the fossil record forever.

The Mystery of the Puzzling Puddles

Most of the anomalies in this book fall into readily classifiable types: ghosts, water monsters, UFOs, haunted houses, psychic experiences and so on.

But occasionally something so monumentally strange comes along that it's completely unclassifiable.

Such an event occurred in a Windsor home in 1955.

A physician, his wife and their two daughters had lived for nine years in their comfortable and attractive two-story house on Cherry Street. There was nothing odd about the house itself. In fact, it could not have been more normal, with its brown and white shingled exterior and attached garage.

But starting on Monday, September 20, 1955, normalcy became a thing of the past as the family plunged headlong into Vermont's own version of The Twilight Zone.

On that day, one of the daughters noticed that a quantity of water had collected in the concave seat of a wooden chair in her bedroom. As she was about to clean it up, she noticed a second puddle on the floor. Where had it come from? Nothing had spilled. Nothing was leaking—it wasn't raining outside and no water pipes ran through her room.

No sooner had she told her mother than other family members started to notice pools of water here and there on the first and second floors of the house.

What started as a trickle soon became a downpour. Over the first two days, they collected thirteen pails of water. But no one could determine where it was coming from—it just seemed to appear.

This water from nowhere saturated the contents of their bureau drawers. Clothes hanging in closets were soaked and dripping onto the floor. Dishes, cups and glasses in kitchen cupboards filled with water. Continual mopping and sponging was useless; it was like trying to bail out a sinking ship.

Mattresses, pillows and living room furniture got so wet they had to be removed from the house.

The doctor called in friends and neighbors hoping someone could make sense of this unique water problem. The puzzled Windsorites looked around, scratched their heads, shrugged, and observed that the air didn't *seem* to be unusually warm. Or cold. Or damp. They didn't notice any mist or haze. And they could discern no possible source for the accumulating water. The neighbors were also quick to point out that nothing remotely similar was going on in any of their houses nearby.

Yet water continued to appear. In drawers. Bowls. Dishes. On chairs and all over the floor. The *Claremont (N.H.) Daily Eagle* reported that, on occasion, it actually rained inside the house!

The doctor described one instance when he was carrying a bowl of grapes from the kitchen. By the time he got to the living room, the bowl had filled with water almost in front of his eyes.

The family called in various experts hoping to get to the bottom of things: electricians, building contractors, plumbers, insulation installers, furnace specialists—even a dowser, but no one could offer a realistic explanation. However, the baffled experts did make a few interesting observations: there were no broken water lines or sweating pipes; there was no problem with ground water or seepage from a well or spring. And, perhaps odder still, the walls and ceilings were not afflicted. They, and the insulation *inside* the walls, remained perfectly dry. As did the cellar.

Sometimes things would seem to be drying out, then the family would leave and come home to a house that seemed to have been flooded.

So where was the water coming from?

Why did it seem to just appear before their eyes? And why *now*, after living in the house for nine years with no similar problems?

The doctor said, "To . . . stand in the middle of a room, feeling no dampness, and to watch the water mount on the boards about you, is an experience almost terrifying!"

Things climaxed during the first weekend in October.

Water cascaded from the kitchen cupboards, streamed from under the electric stove and dripped from the living room piano. The family had finally had enough. They had already moved what furniture they wanted to save into the garage, now they too moved out, driven from their home by the fantastic flood.

All four moved into a trailer in their front yard. Where—it may be important to note—the phenomenon did not follow.

Of course the Associated Press picked up the story and soon newspapers from all around the world were phoning to get more information. Letters with questions, explanations and prayers arrived almost every day. Endless lines of curiosity seekers paraded by the house on foot and in cars. Numerous eccentrics imposed themselves into the situation with scenarios involving demonic or divine intervention.

Then, about a month after the phenomenon started, it stopped. The end, like the beginning, came without explanation. In hopes of cutting off the flow of curiosity seekers, the doctor issued a press release saying the problem had been solved. But it hadn't been solved—it just stopped.

Over the weekend of October 22 and 23, the family began moving back into their house. And eventually life returned to normal.

Or as normal as it could ever be after experiencing something of such high strangeness.

When I reflect on stories like this one it almost makes me believe there really is some sort of cosmic joker who enjoys involving unsuspecting souls in outlandish antics such as these.

And if this was a cosmic joke, I should close by telling you the punch line.

You may have noticed that so far I haven't mentioned the name of the unfortunate family. Believe it or not, it was Waterman.

The Mystery of the Graye Area

WHO WAS THE FIRST EUROPEAN TO SET FOOT IN VERMONT? Well, there are many theories—a Viking, a Celt, a Phoenician—but "first" status is traditionally awarded to the earliest explorer to leave a written record of his arrival. On that basis, the French explorer Samuel de Champlain wins hands down. In 1609, he made his way south into the lake that now bears his name. Of this there can be no doubt; he left his diaries to prove it.

But there is another document that might prove someone got here before Champlain. An Englishman. Sadly, he didn't live long enough to tell the tale.

On a wintry December day in 1853, two Vermonters—Orlando Green and P. R. Ripley of Swanton—were shoveling sand near the bank of the Missisquoi River. The sand was to be used in the Swanton Falls marble plant where they worked.

Six to twelve inches down, embedded in a sturdy piece of sod, they saw something that should not have been there. It was a gray metallic tube about 5 inches long. The tube was fashioned from an irregular piece of lead, apparently molded around a stick, and sealed at both ends with a brittle white substance.

Understandably curious, Green and Ripley opened the tube. Inside, they found a piece of heavy paper. With some difficulty, they were able to make out a message written in what appeared to be archaic English. Here, in its entirety, is what the message said in one long sentence:

> This is the Solme day I must now die this is the
> 90th day since we left the Ship all are Perished
> and on the Banks of this River I die to, farewelle
> may future posteretye know our end

It was signed Johne Graye (or possibly Johne Greye or Johne Gedge, the handwriting makes it difficult to say) and dated November 29, 1564.

So who was Johne Graye? How did he get here? And what was he doing on the Missisquoi River some forty-five years before Champlain arrived?

The first historian to examine the tube and its contents was the Reverend John B. Perry of Swanton. Experts agreed he was well-suited for the job and—with the help of a history professor and an assayer from Boston—Perry declared that tube, paper and message were genuine.

Perry's theory was that Johne Graye had been a member of one of Sir Martin Frobisher's expeditions to discover the Northwest Passage. Perhaps Graye and the other men were part of a scouting party that got lost. Or maybe they had been put ashore to fend for themselves when the ship's supplies ran low. But Reverend Perry was not able to substantiate his theory. He couldn't find any record of a Frobisher expedition that corresponded to the time frame in Graye's note. Surprisingly, he located a record showing that Frobisher *did* put five men ashore in 1576. But that was twelve years off. The dates just didn't work out right.

Although dates couldn't prove the message was on the level, they couldn't *disprove* anything. The numbers could have been copied incorrectly on historical documents. Or Graye could have come from one of the many expeditions for which there is no existing record.

And maybe Graye and his men *didn't* come from Frobisher's ship. After all, there was really no internal evidence to suggest the doomed sailors had been making their way south. They *could* have been heading north from the Hudson River.

Over the years, the controversy about Green and Ripley's baffling discovery has pretty much died out. Occasionally, curious historians will look into it with some interest, but opinions continue to differ.

As far as I know, the most recent investigation was in 1964, four hundred years after the date on the message.

The investigator, Walter Hard Jr., then the editor of *Vermont Life* Magazine, concluded that the message was a hoax. He determined that the handwriting was not sufficiently ancient, that there were no recorded expeditions in 1564, and, perhaps most vexing, he reported that the original document and its container had disappeared.

Today modern investigative techniques might shed definitive light on the mystery, but the evidence is gone. For years we've known that a facsimile of the paper was maintained at the Highgate Library. But the whereabouts of the original, the origin of Johne Graye, and the circumstances of his lonely death will remain one haunting episode of Vermont's many unsolved mysteries.

The Mystery of the Copper Seekers

IN SPITE OF ALL THE EVIDENCE TO THE CONTRARY, many people still give Christopher Columbus credit for discovering America. And they say the Pilgrims were first to settle New England. Yet even when I was in school, we knew the Vikings got here earlier; their temporary settlements are marked by posthole patterns and a scattering of artifacts.

More locally, some mavericks may still favor Johne Graye over Champlain as discoverer of Vermont.

But there is evidence that Columbus, the Pilgrims, Champlain, Johne Graye, and even the Vikings may not have been the very first non-native Americans to discover, and even settle, in New England.

Right here in the Green Mountains there is the possibility of pre-Columbian, even pre-Viking, colonization.

My personal involvement with this particular mystery started around 1965 when my friend Rick Bates and I were hiking in the woods behind my family place in Chester.

We saw what appeared to be a mound of earth, roughly 10 feet high, grassed-over and patchy with small trees and shrubbery. The

mound didn't look unusual at all until we walked around it . . . and discovered an opening!

From this viewpoint, the structure looked more like an igloo, made not of ice but of stone. The interior walls were fitted rocks, without mortar; the roof was massive stone slabs that must have weighed several tons.

The unfamiliar structure gave us a weird feeling because we had no idea what it was. Sure, we were used to seeing things made of stone. A couple of Vermont boys, we'd grown up in houses with stone foundations surrounded by miles of stone walls. In fact our hometown, Chester, was renowned for its beautiful stone buildings.

But this building was different. What could it be? A crypt? A storage bin? An abandoned mine? What?

It wasn't until much later that I discovered Chester's stone structure—and 50 others like it around the state—are controversial: No one knows for sure who made them. Or when. Or why.

And what are the strange markings on many of them?

And who's responsible for the carved faces, inscriptions and fertility stones found near many of these odd chambers?

Mainstream archaeologists, including our state archaeologist Giovanna Peebles, insist these igloo-like sites are nothing more romantic than Colonial root cellars. The markings, they say, are merely scrapes from passing glaciers or the scars of Colonial plows.

Other archaeologists, however, have different theories. The late Dr. Warren Cook of Castleton State College was one of a number of scholars who feel the sites indicate ancient settlements.

Cook theorized that much of Vermont and parts of New England had actually been colonized by sea-going Celts during the Bronze Age when European supplies of copper appeared to be dwindling. In other words, Cook believed Vermont was full of mining settlements built and populated by ancient Celtic copper-seekers. And why not? Our state is loaded with copper; we were the country's leading producer during the Civil War.

Vermont may have been settled by Europeans at least 2,000 years before Columbus! Celts who worshipped the Earth Mother, Bianu, and the sun god, Bel.

Some speculate that Vermont's mysterious stone sites might well be religious structures, shrines or communal mausoleums, places for returning the ashes of the dead to the womb of Mother Earth. Some *have* been shown to have astronomical significance. Just like Stonehenge in England, there is confirmed astronomical alignment during solstices and equinoxes.

And the strange organized markings—short lines growing from or bisecting longer lines—etched on their walls, what of them? They might be a language called Ogam. Ogam script has been discovered on similar structures in Europe—and has been translated!

If that is so, perhaps retired Harvard professor Barry Fell's reading of an inscribed stone in Royalton contains Vermont's original name. The Ogam inscription calls Vermont: "Precincts of the gods of the land beyond the sunset."

The Mystery of the Deadly Conspirators

VERMONT'S DARKEST MYSTERY may also be our best-kept secret. It involves a mysterious disappearance, a death, manipulation of justice and a conspiracy that has lasted until this very day. The chilling details of what happened in postcard-perfect Newbury quickly spread from regional to international newspapers, reaching as far away as Glasgow, London, even Moscow.

Events began on December 31, 1957, at 3:30 in the morning when one of the town's most successful dairy farmers, 47-year-old Orville A. Gibson, woke up as usual. At 4:00 a.m.—as always—he would begin the day's milking. Gibson grabbed his milking pail, walked across the road to his barn, entered, turned on the lights . . . and vanished!

His wife, Evalyn, waited almost three hours before she called the police.

The two state troopers assigned to Orange County, William Graham and Lawrence Washburn, arrived around 8:00 a.m. Their first thought was suicide, a common death among Vermont dairy farmers at the time.

But when they checked the barn, they found a battered milk pail, scuff marks on the floor and a trail that looked as if something heavy had been dragged. A sack of grain perhaps? Or maybe a body?

Now the troopers suspected Gibson had been kidnapped, maybe murdered. But why?

By 10:00 a.m., the news had spread all over town. Every citizen had a comment or a theory.

Most suspected some kind of revenge scenario tied to an incident that had happened a few days earlier. Gibson—known to some for his bad temper—had been accused of beating his diminutive hired hand, Eri Martin, for accidentally spilling two 40-quart cans of milk. The *rumor* held that Martin was in the hospital, near death, with broken ribs and a damaged kidney. The *truth* was that Martin was perfectly all right; he'd never even been to the hospital.

Gibson's friends said there was no way the God-fearing, hard-working farmer could hurt anybody, that the marks of Martin's "beating" were the result of a drunken fall against the handle of a wheelbarrow. In fact, the hired man admitted this was so.

But another faction in town—one that included high-placed, influential people—hated Gibson. They envied his success, his shrewd business dealings and his lifelong status as a "model citizen." Perhaps long-held resentments inspired thoughts of vengeance. Eri Martin's alleged beating was most probably an excuse—not the motive—for the suspected kidnapping.

The "revenge" theory strengthened when police found bits of silage on an iron bridge over the Connecticut River—silage from Orville Gibson's barn. Troopers Graham and Washburn stepped up their investigation—dragging the river, interviewing citizens, searching grain bins and manure piles, even consulting a Plainfield psychic—but they found no more useful evidence.

Then in March, three months after his disappearance, Gibson's body bobbed to the surface of the Connecticut River. Any lingering notions of suicide were quickly abandoned: Gibson's corpse was securely trussed up, wrists tied beneath his thighs, then secured to his tightly bound ankles.

Before the investigation could proceed, an interesting legal question had to be answered. The low-water mark on the Connecticut's Vermont shore is the boundary line between Vermont and New Hampshire. So if there were water in Gibson's lungs, then, technically, he had drowned in New Hampshire. In consequence, the murder would have to be handled by New Hampshire courts.

If Gibson hadn't drowned, then most likely he had been murdered in Vermont before his dead body was tossed into New Hampshire waters.

Dr. Richard Woodruff, the medical examiner, ruled in favor of Vermont, and the investigation proceeded.

Hordes of townspeople were questioned. Eighty individuals agreed to take lie-detector tests. In fact, one polygraph machine broke down because of constant use. The interviews turned up a lot of interesting, in some cases scandalous, information, but they never revealed who killed Gibson.

Eventually, two local men—Ozzie Welch, the high school janitor, and Frank Carpenter, a drunken brawler—were arraigned and tried separately for the murder.

At Welch's trial, a local doctor, John Perry Hooker, testified that he had treated Welch for a good many years. On the evening in question, Hooker had seen the accused and several others in a car parked 100 yards south of Gibson's barn. The time: fifteen minutes before the farmer vanished. He also thought he recognized Carpenter *and* the vehicle, a 1953 two-toned Kaiser sedan. That automobile, and the rope from Gibson's corpse, were directly linked to Ozzie Welch.

Then a new weirdness began:

The prosecution presented twenty-eight witnesses. The defense presented no one. Ozzie Welch didn't even take the stand on his own behalf. Not one shred of defensive evidence was offered, yet, oddly, the judge directed the jury to find Welch not guilty.

Odder still, at Frank Carpenter's trial, important witnesses, including Dr. Hooker, suddenly became vague in their testimony. Several recanted their written statements. Now, with the prosecution's case severely weakened, Carpenter also went free.

So what happened? What caused such a mysterious turnaround? Was this pure Vermont justice, or was something untoward going on behind the scenes?

Let's review the situation:

The murder had dramatically polarized the town, dividing inhabitants into two distinct groups: relatives and friends of the dead man and relatives and friends of the accused and suspected murderers.

Many of his detractors begrudged Orville Gibson his lifelong success. Folks who'd grown up with him recalled that even as a lad, Gibson had been conspicuously successful: he got the best marks in school, eventually becoming valedictorian of his graduating class. Then, and as an adult, he remained ambitious and independent, never becoming "one of the boys," nor indulging in smoking, drinking or perpetuating local gossip. He breezed through the Great Depression as a traveling salesman for the wholesale grocery firm of Church & Dwight. Later, he outfoxed some prominent neighbors when he bought the 300-acre dairy farm that he christened "Bonnie Acres."

By 1957, Orville and Evalyn Gibson had made their farm into one of the finest in the state, a showpiece. They had 100 head of cattle, most of them purebred Holsteins, and an impressive supply of expensive farm machinery, most of it paid for.

Such success inevitably inspires envy and resentment. And such ignoble emotions, festering for years, can serve as strong motives.

The most common theory explaining Orville Gibson's murder is that a bunch of local good-ol'-boys got liquored-up and decided to give Gibson a scare, using the alleged "beating" of Eri Martin as an excuse for action. Fueled by whiskey, rivalry and self-righteous wrath, violence erupted. Four or more men jumped him, tied him up and planned to humiliate him by dumping him on the village green. But the *way* they tied him cut off his air supply. He died of suffocation in the trunk of the car. Upon discovering what had happened, the kidnappers probably panicked and threw his lifeless body into the river.

But how do we explain the not-guilty verdict and the town's nearly four decades of silence? Maybe like this: say ten or more men hatched the revenge plot. Each had an endless network of friends, family and associates in the area. In effect, everyone in Newbury was connected to everyone else. And some of those connections wielded power and influence.

But someone knew who murdered Orville Gibson.

And someone still does.

Principals in the case have long ago died off or moved away. The chief investigators have retired, the reporters moved on to other things. Though a substantial reward is still offered for clues leading to a solution to Vermont's most shameful mystery, nothing new has come forth in many years. As of today, all the work of two devoted state police officers and a small army of investigators has come to nothing, short-circuited by what may be a cover-up and a conspiracy of silence that has lasted nearly forty years.

As one Newbury woman said, "What's amazing to me is that all those people could have been quiet for so long. It's either a compliment to the Vermont character or a sad commentary."

The Mystery of the Bennington Triangle

IN THIS FINAL AND PERHAPS MOST BAFFLING MYSTERY, we return to one of the most untamed places in Vermont—the wilderness of Glastenbury Mountain.

As you may recall, it is considered a haunted place, a place with a "reputation." Since pre-Colonial times Glastenbury's remote and sometimes inaccessible slopes have given birth to strange tales of mysterious lights, untraceable sounds and unidentifiable odors.

Even the Indians shunned the place. Because winds from all four directions met on the mountain, they believed the area was cursed. They refused to live there and saw the land as suitable only for burying their dead.

The few Colonial families who settled there were plagued by misfortune. Many suffered recurring bouts of disease; mothers died in childbirth; and madness seemed to claim more than its share of victims.

There, specters skulked among the trees. And unknown creatures—glimpsed fleetingly along thickly wooded pathways or deep within the silent swampland—burned themselves forever into memory.

It was there we encountered the baffling "Bennington Monster" and witnessed its attack on a stagecoach passing along the mountainous ridges from Woodford. It was there in 1892 that madman Henry MacDowell was sentenced to life in the Waterbury Asylum for murdering Jim Crowley. But he escaped and vanished. Some people say he returned to the Glastenbury slopes where he remains to this day.

But all this happened a long time ago.

What of today? Do the mountains remain as mysterious? Are dark tales still told?

And what should we make of all these reports of spirits and curses and monsters? Could there possibly be any truth to any of it?

Well, of course, it depends on whom you talk to. But there's one thing we know for sure: the Glastenbury Mountain area is where one of Vermont's most tragic and frightening mysteries took place. And not too very long ago. The events were covered locally—in the *Bennington Banner,* the *Rutland Herald,* the *Burlington Free Press* and in many out-of-state papers.

I call the site of these strange events "The Bennington Triangle" because of the unexplained disappearances—perhaps ten in all—that began in the Glastenbury Mountain area in late 1945. To this day, not one of them has been solved. In fact, no one has ever uncovered so much as a clue.

The strangeness started with a man named Middie Rivers, a 74-year-old native of the region. It is worth noting that Rivers had long worked as a hunting and fishing guide, so we may safely assume he knew the area very well. Also, he was in perfect health according to a recent physical.

The weather was unusually mild on November 12, 1945, as Rivers led four hunters up onto the mountain. All was uneventful until they started to return to their camp in Bickford Hollow just off Long Trail Road and not far from the Route 9 entrance to the trail itself.

Rivers got a bit ahead of the others. They never caught up with him. The old man vanished completely.

Volunteers and police combed the area for hours. They maintained hope by reminding each other that Rivers was an experienced woodsman and would know how to survive in the wild. Expanded efforts, led by fire chief Wallace Mattison, continued for a month. Selectmen even offered to pay searchers to keep the hunt going. And a psychic, Clara Jepson of Bennington, was consulted, but her vision proved inaccurate. No trace—nothing—was ever found.

A young woman named Paula Welden was the second to go. (It was this mysterious, highly publicized case more than any other single event that demonstrated the need for and led to the establishment of the Vermont State Police.)

On Sunday, December 1, 1946, this 18-year-old sophomore from Dewey Hall at Bennington College set out for a short afternoon hike on the Long Trail.

A driver picked her up on Route 67A and gave her a ride along Route 9 as far as his home in Woodford Hollow. About 4:00 p.m., she was spotted by Ernest Whitman, an employee of the *Bennington Banner*. She asked Whitman directions to the Long Trail and he told her it was just a short walk away. Later, other witnesses saw her on the trail.

The five-foot five blonde was easy to see and identify because of the red parka she wore with her blue jeans and sneakers.

When Monday afternoon came, Paula hadn't returned to school. The college called the Sheriff's Department, which was joined by 400 students, faculty and townspeople. They searched diligently but found nothing.

Governor Ernest Gibson called in the FBI, which was assisted by New York and Connecticut state police.

Search parties combed the area for weeks. The Long Trail was thoroughly inspected as was the Woodford Hollow area. They searched around the Glastenbury fire tower and crossed from Glastenbury to Bald

Mountain. In spite of their efforts, a $5,000 reward, and the aid of a famous clairvoyant, not a single clue turned up. The official search—involving bloodhounds, airplanes, helicopters and well over 1,000 people—ended on December 22 with no results.

No sign of a body. No clothing. No evidence at all. The only thing certain is that a young woman took a walk in the Vermont hills and never came back.

Oddly, the third person vanished on the third anniversary of Paula Welden's disappearance. It was three years to the day: December 1, 1949. This was the elderly James E. Tetford who'd been visiting relatives in the northern Vermont towns of Cambridge and Franklin. His family put him on a bus in St. Albans and waved good-by as he started back to the Bennington Soldiers Home where he lived. He was never to arrive.

The exact location of his disappearance is obscured by the event's strangeness. Witnesses saw him get on the bus. He was aboard at the stop before Bennington. But, weird as it sounds, he apparently never got off! Again, no one saw anything; there were no clues. Even the bus driver couldn't offer an explanation.

On Columbus Day of 1950 it was Paul Jepson's turn. Paul was just a kid, only 8 years old. His mother and father, former high school teachers, owned a farm in North Bennington on White Creek Road. Along with raising cows and pigs, they served as caretakers for the town dump on East Road. That's where the tragedy occurred.

Paul was at the dump, waiting in the pickup, while his mother relocated some pigs. He was but briefly unattended. Sometime between 3:00 and 4:00 p.m., Mom looked up and Paul was gone.

He should have been easy to spot because he wore a red jacket under the shoulder straps of his brown overalls.

But Mrs. Jepson couldn't see him and eventually called for help.

Again, well-practiced volunteers assembled to begin a search.

Paul's father disclosed an odd bit of information. He said that lately Paul had had an unexplained "yen" to go into the mountains.

Hundreds of civilians joined officials to search the dump, the road and the mountains. They used Coast Guard planes and bloodhounds borrowed from the New Hampshire State Police. This time they instituted a "double check" system; as soon as one group finished searching an area, a second group would search the same area.

Again, local psychics proved useless.

Again, nothing was found.

One local legend holds that the bloodhounds lost Paul's scent at the exact spot where Paula Welden was last seen. The truth is that Paul's trail stopped when the bloodhounds lost him at the junction of East and Chapel Roads, to the west of Glastenbury and Bald Mountains.

On October 14, 1950, the *Bennington Banner* reported, "The mystery of Paul's complete disappearance, and not a single clue to work on, makes the third [fourth, counting Tetford] such case of a missing person in practically the same area during the past five years."

A pattern definitely seemed to be emerging.

About two weeks later, on Saturday, October 28, another woman, Freida Langer, was on a hike with her cousin Herbert Elsner. They had left from their family camp on the eastern side of Glastenbury Mountain, just off the road near Somerset Reservoir.

Freida, a short, rugged woman of 53, was known as an experienced gun-handler and woodsperson. She was completely familiar with the area.

At about 3:45 p.m., only about a half mile from camp, she slipped and fell into a stream. She told her cousin that she would run the short distance back to the camp, change clothes and hurry back to join him.

When she didn't return, Herbert went to look for her. Not only had she not reached camp, no one saw her come out of the woods. Alarmed by another disappearance in the same general area, local officials quickly launched another search. It turned up nothing.

Forces regrouped and initiated a second search on November 1. General Merritt Edson, state director of public safety, issued an emphatic command. He ordered the officers to stay on the job until they found Langer dead or alive, or some satisfactory explanation of her disappearance. This involved helicopters, amphibious planes and hordes of people on foot. But Edson couldn't command his men to do the impossible. This search, too, ended in frustration.

There were a lot of mysterious components to Freida Langer's disappearance. One seemed especially troubling, as pointed out by the *Bennington Banner.* "One of the things hard to explain is how Mrs. Langer could have become so completely lost in an hour's time before dark in an area with which she was so thoroughly familiar." Remember, when last seen she was headed toward their camp which was less than half a mile away. Also, there was plenty of daylight left for such a short, quick walk.

On November 5, the searchers tried again. They divided into three groups of thirty, then lined up and marched side by side. It would have been hard to miss a clue if one had been there to find. It was a good plan, but it failed to turn up anything at all.

On Tuesday, November 7, State's Attorney Edward John and Governor Harold Arthur again stressed General Edson's order, "Get out and find that body!" Though limited searching went on nonstop, a huge weekend search was planned for November 11 and 12. It was the biggest ever. Sportsmen and military units joined police, firemen and community volunteers. Over 300 people literally scoured the woods.

And found nothing.

On the Monday following this monumental effort, Freida's husband, Max, and cousin Herbert finally gave up hope.

What did the combined forces of military and civilian searchers have to show for all their efforts of the last two weeks? Not one single worthwhile clue.

Three of the sources I used in preparing this chapter include at least two more disappearances in "The Bennington Triangle."

On December 3, 1950, only a few days after the search for Freida Langer ended, Frances Christman left her home to visit a friend whose house was just a half mile away. It was a dark night and snowing hard. Somewhere on that brief hike, she vanished without a trace.

I returned to the source material and was able to verify that this story was reported in the Bennington newspaper. And the woman did vanish. However, researchers either didn't know Vermont geography, or they just didn't read the newspapers very well. For Frances Christman disappeared from her home in Hinesburg, a good 120 miles north of the Glastenbury area.

And there's more. Several accounts of the Glastenbury tragedy include the disappearance of teenager Martha Jeanette Jones. She vanished on November 13, 1950.

Martha actually came up missing before Frances Christman, but, in spite of all that had gone on before, her mother did not report her absence right away; she assumed the girl had run off with her boyfriend.

Martha, known as "Mitzi," was seen hitchhiking between her Bondville home and Manchester, where she went to school. This would put her on Route 30, which bisects the vast Green Mountain National Forest tract that includes Glastenbury Mountain.

So she was much closer to the Bennington Triangle than Christman. However, if the researcher(s) had kept flipping pages of old newspapers they would have discovered that Mitzi's mother had been right all along. According to the December 20, 1950 issue of the *Bennington Banner*, Mitzi turned up in Accotink, Virginia, near a military base, working as a waitress.

Think about it.

Even if we subtract Christman and Jones, that leaves five human beings who vanished between 1945 and 1950. Vanished without a trace. Where did they go? How can we possibly explain something like this?

Could the Bennington Monster have carried them off into the caves and swamps of Glastenbury Mountain? Could they have slipped through some vile vortex, some interdimensional trap door like the one referred to as the Bermuda Triangle, famous for gobbling up planes and ships that are never seen again?

Or maybe they encountered an enchanted stone in the White Rocks section of the Glastenbury Range, a stone known to the Indians as one that yawns and swallows anyone who steps on it?

One *Banner* reporter even speculated that there exists something of a Yankee Shangri-La in the Glastenbury area, a lost horizon into which people inadvertently step, never to be seen again. To some that probably seems the best explanation because it discounts other less happy endings.

For example, in recent years there's been a lot of talk about human beings who are abducted by UFOs. Some, under hypnosis, claim to have been victims of sinister medical examinations, then released with holes in their memories and implants in their brains. Some, I suppose, never come back at all.

Perhaps the answer is more prosaic, something not precisely identified in the annals of American crime circa 1945—the serial killer.

All we know for sure is that the mysterious events around Bennington took place over a limited amount of time: five years. And in roughly the same area—on or near the Long Trail between the summit of Glastenbury Mountain and the trail's intersection with Route 9. They occurred during the last three months of the calendar year. Then they stopped.

Serial killers operate that way; they do their dirty work, then drift from place to place. Maybe the perpetrator was someone who visited Vermont in October, November and December. Maybe for hunting season, or the holidays.

The victims' ages spanned from 8 to 75. They were about equally divided between men and women. Perhaps this absence of pattern argues against the serial killer idea.

Even at the time, local fears were personified by the invention of a particularly cunning madman. To explain the mysterious events, Bennington citizens created a hypothetical slayer alternately known as "The Bennington Ripper" or "The Mad Murderer of the Long Trail."

But the truth is, no murder was ever proven. Maybe the answer to the mystery still lies buried in some unmarked grave with some undiscovered corpse.

And all these complex questions are counterbalanced by others that are deceptively simple.

Like why didn't the snow on the ground during the months of these vanishings facilitate the searches?

And if some of the victims wandered off and froze to death, why didn't the spring thaw expose their remains?

One can't help but wonder if the disappearances have stopped altogether. Or have there been related vanishings in the Glastenbury area that could be uncovered with just a little digging?

In a *Burlington Free Press* article dated October 25, 1981, reporter Sally Jacobs says that two years after the Paula Welden disappearance, "a trio of hunters from Massachusetts vanished near Glastenbury [the unincorporated ghost town on Glastenbury Mountain]. Their disappearance, like those that preceded them, remains a mystery."

And one of the *Banner* articles I reviewed made reference to a 13-year-old boy, Melvin Hills of Bennington, who was lost in the same area around October 11, 1942.

If these are true, then the number of disappearances goes from five to nine.

More victims, but no less a puzzle.

There are a couple of chilling footnotes to the story.

On May 12, 1951, the dead body of Freida Langer did appear, *seven months after she'd vanished*. Impossibly, the corpse was found among tall grasses near the flood dam of Somerset Reservoir. It was in an open, visible area where searchers simply could not have missed it. Remember, teams had repeatedly combed the area for weeks. The search for Freida Langer was, arguably, the most thorough of all.

Unfortunately, Langer's fate couldn't be determined by examining the remains; as the *Banner* said, they were in "gruesome condition."

And what of the others? No human remains were ever found. No thread of clothing. No blood. No hair. No clue at all. Not even a ransom note.

The last weird but minor postscript is this: researcher Bruce Hallenbeck from Valatie, New York, told me that of the half dozen or so photographs of "monsters" taken in Vermont, one was taken in the vicinity of Glastenbury Mountain. It shows a big, dark, hulking form partly hidden among green forest vegetation. Hallenbeck claims it's the photo of a Bigfoot.

It is still visible for leagues across the river, veiled in distance and golden with elfin light. The spell of the past has not departed, for Vermont has given us something that we have always sought, and that can never be effaced from our spirit. Dim on the horizon the purpling hills rise, Ascutney towering in lordship above its neighbors. A bend shuts it from sight, and we are alone with our meditations.

—H. P. Lovecraft
Vermont—A First Impression

Sources

IN BOOKS ABOUT GHOSTS, goblins, and other "strange-but-maybe-true" phenomena, Vermont is routinely ignored. Tomes with promising titles like *Yankee Ghosts*, *New England's Legends and Folk Lore*, and *America's Haunted Houses* usually contain nothing about Vermont. You could get the idea nothing weird ever happens here.

On the other hand, I have found Vermont to be a virtually unmined source of high strangeness. Finding the gems, however, can take a good deal of prospecting. That's partly because no publication, with the notable exception of *Vermont Life* Magazine's *Mischief in the Mountains*, has ever been totally devoted to strange Vermont lore. Consequently, putting together this book has been a little like putting together a rock collection. Amid the marble, granite and schist, I unearthed a few precious stones.

So where did I dig up all these treasures?

It might be difficult to reconstruct all the sources; there are so many. I've been gathering these tales all my life, but not in any systematic way—a clipping here, a scribbled note there, a half-recalled anecdote overheard in someone else's conversation . . .

Day-to-day living in Vermont has exposed me to many stories, enough to conclude the majority have never been put on paper. To complicate things further, most tales, whether in print or not, exist in more than one form.

For example, I have known about Phineas Gage's railroad accident for most of my life. I grew up in the town bordering Cavendish. In that neck of the woods, Phineas and his crowbar have been in the oral tradition for a century. The version I heard in my youth had Phineas picking himself up after the explosion with the crowbar still embedded in his skull—protruding on both sides.

The unnamed doctors, feeling it would be too dangerous to remove it, cut off both ends tight to his skull, let skin grow over them, and allowed Phineas to spend the rest of his life walking around with an iron bar in his head. Variations of the story have appeared in several publications—including several journals of psychology. Interestingly, no two versions are identical. My retelling is a best-guess effort but is by no means definitive.

And that is the nature of folktales in general: each teller customizes a story to best fit his or her audience or personal storytelling style. Infusing a tale with drama and suspense requires creativity; it's human nature to fabricate details when knowledge is incomplete. The result? Fact and fancy get hopelessly entangled. To the historian, it's a nightmare; to the yarn-spinner, it's business as usual.

Many of the stories in this book came to me in fragments, and I had to try to piece them together. Many I discovered while looking for other things. And many were recorded in books, magazines and newspapers and readily available. When stories were in books, I was generally able to locate more than one version. Things published in newspapers were often one-of-a-kind.

Probably the three most productive sources of Vermont lore are *Vermont Life* Magazine, *Green Mountain Whittlin's* (a publication of the Vermont Folklore Society) and local newspapers, especially around Halloween.

Town histories are often good places for prospecting, as is Abby Hemenway's *Vermont Historical Gazetteer* and the late Leon Dean's column in *Vermont Quarterly* and later, *Vermont History*. But I have yet to strike the mother lode. The closest I've found is Richard Sweterlitsch's folklore archives in Special Collections at the University of Vermont library.

There are a few useful books in addition to *Mischief*: Col. Olcott's *People from the Other World*, most anything by Robert Pike; the ghost story collections of James Reynolds; Joe Zarzynski's various books on Champ; *Those Eccentric Yankees* and *Mysterious New England* from Yankee Books; most of Robert Ellis Cahill's New England series; Alton H. Blackington's "Yankee Yarns" collections, and, as mentioned in the text, Lee Dana Goodman's entertaining *Vermont Saints and Sinners*.

A partial list of other reference books includes: Doyle's *History of Spiritualism* and *The Edge of the Unknown*; Major Donald Keyhoe's *Aliens From Space*; Gerald McFarland's *The Counterfeit Man*; Jerome Clark's *Unexplained!*; Meurger and Gagnon's *Lake Monster Traditions*; B.A Botkin's *Treasury of New England Folklore*; Richard M. Dorson's *Jonathan Draws the Long Bow*; *Stranger than Science* and *Strange World* by Frank Edwards; *Incident at Exeter* by John C Fuller; *Haunted New England* by Eastman and Bolte; *The Ghostly Gazetteer* by Arthur Myers; *Into Thin Air* by Paul Begg; *Covered Bridges of Lamoille County* by R.J. Hagerman; Barry Fell's *America B.C.*; Warren Cook's *Ancient Vermont*; *Legacy of the Lake* by Jane C. Beck; *Vampires, Burial, and Death* by Paul Barber; the delightful *Over Their Dead Bodies* by Thomas C. Mann and Janet Greene. And the list goes on . . .

I am indebted to several people who were kind enough to share their unpublished papers, among them: Greg Guma's work on the Eddy Brothers; Dr. Thomas Altherr's paper on big cat sightings; a manuscript called "Monsters of the Northwoods" by Robert and Paul Bartholomew, William Brann and Bruce Hallenbeck; and a history of the Vermont State Police by Michael J. Carpenter.

The newspapers I used include, but are not limited to: the *Rutland Herald, Burlington Free Press, Bennington Banner, Newport Daily Express, Barre-Montpelier Times Argus, Claremont [NH] Daily Eagle, Vermont Journal,* the *New York Times, County Courier, Brattleboro Reformer* and *Vermont Vanguard.*

A few magazines were consulted to some degree: *Window of Vermont, Yankee, Fate, Strange, Omni,* and the invaluable *Champ Channels.*

In short, I keep my eyes and ears open; you can find this kind of stuff almost anywhere.

Before closing, I'd like to thank the following people. Each helped in some way with this project: Jim and Chris DeFilippi, Stephen R. Bissette, K.K. Wilder, Barry Estabrook, Alice Lawrence, William Pratt, Tom Slayton, Howard Frank Mosher, Betty Smith, Sam Sanders and the folks at Vermont Public Radio, Ed Hyde, Jacques Boisvert, Barbara Malloy, Kathleen MacDonald, Jules Older, Paul Barror, Seth Steinzor, Paul Bartholomew, R. Caine, Charles Johnson, Charlie Powell, Janet Hopper, Greg Guma, John Coon, Abe Stoker, Joanie Kemsley,

Paul Mascitti, Melissa Cook, Wes Chester, Joe Chaput, Joseph W. Zarzynski, Bill Schubart, Stefan Hard, Jane Beck and the folks at the Vermont Folklife Center, P. M. Daniels, U. N. Owen, Roderick G. Bates, Arlene Tarantino, Michael Shea and Capt. Frank Shea and all those who, by request or oversight, shall remain anonymous. My sincerest apologies to anyone I've forgotten.

Alas, the job is still not done. In spite of all this help and all these sources, I was unable to find anything about: *Aunt Sally*, the phantom steamship on Lake Morey; the Native American ghosts who supposedly haunt Lincoln Gap; a violent spirit on one of the Champlain Islands; a mysterious fire anomaly in Woodstock; and a Vermont case of Spontaneous Human Combustion. I'll get right to work on those for Volume Two . . .